The Less Developed Countries
and the World Trading System

Studies in International Political Economy will present new work, from a multinational stable of authors, on major issues, theoretical and practical, in the international political economy.

General Editor

Susan Strange, Professor of International Relations, London School of Economics and Political Science, England

Consulting Editors

Ladd Hollist, Visiting Associate Professor, Brigham Young University, USA

Karl Kaiser, Director, Research Institute of the German Society for Foreign Affairs, Bonn, and Professor of Political Science, University of Cologne, West Germany

William Leohr, Graduate School of International Studies, University of Denver, USA

Joseph Nye, Professor of Government, Harvard University, USA

Already Published

The Political Economy of New and Old Industrial Countries
The East European Economies in the 1970s
Defence, Technology and International Integration
Japan and Western Europe
Tax Havens and Offshore Finance
The North–South Dialogue
The International Gold Standard
Transnational Oil
Defending Europe in the 1990s
Forming Economic Policy

Forthcoming Titles

Dependency Transformed

The Less Developed Countries and the World Trading System

A Challenge to the GATT

Diana Tussie

St. Martin's Press, New York

First published in the United States of America in 1987.

Library of Congress Cataloging in Publication data
Tussie, Diana.
   The less developed countries and the world
trading system.
   Bibliography: p.
   Includes index.
   1. Tariff—Developing countries.   2. Developing
countries—Commercial policy.   3. Latin America—
Economic integration.   4. Contracting Parties to
the General Agreement on Tariffs and Trade.   I. Title.
HF2580.9.T87   1987   382'.09172'4   86-20399
ISBN 0-312-48158-6

Typeset by Joshua Associates Limited, Oxford
Printed in Great Britain

Contents

Tables

Figures

Preface

This book is about the regulation of international trade. When first reading the literature on the North–South debate I was struck by the paradox that while there are a number of works on the role of the IMF for the developing world, there is no equivalent study of the GATT, even though the debate owes its origins largely to trade problems. Why is it that those who criticize the principles GATT seems to stand for, never bother to delve more deeply into it? Why is the GATT so readily dismissed, yet at the same time governments from the South as well as from the Communist world continue to request accession to it? Why is it neglected in academic circles, while the IMF which could more easily be discarded as a 'capitalist club' receives so much more attention? Is the GATT too difficult a target, or is it such an obvious one that no further analysis is required? There are indeed works on the GATT which touch upon the LDCs' contentions, but apart from the study carried out for the first United Nations Conference on Trade and Development twenty years ago, no major academic work has been dedicated to this subject. Moreover, all the studies on the GATT deal with it outside the boundaries of the North–South debate and have been carried out by economists and lawyers largely sympathetic to the institution.

My journey through these issues was largely inspired by these first thoughts. From them gradually stemmed the conviction that scholars could better serve the wider community they live in by honest and in-depth discussion of the true nature and problems of dependence and domination than by being lured to no purpose either into the rhetoric of confrontation or into wishful thinking. This book is a balancing act between the question posed by my first observations and the ensuing conviction.

Research invariably requires nursing. First and foremost I owe a special debt to the staff and students of the International Relations Department of the London School of Economics. Through the long and lonely hours of gestation I was fortunate to have a constant stream of encouragement and suggestions from Michael Donelan and Susan Strange. To them I owe much of my inspiration. They have provided me with a model of intellectual honesty and clear thinking; to the extent that either of these qualities are embodied in the book, they deserve the major credit. At LSE I also benefited from discussions with Michael Banks, Brian Hindley, Sir Arthur Knight, James Mayal and the

International Political Economy Workshop, where my ideas were first aired. Vincent Cable, Laurence Harris, Hans Singer, Geoffrey Shepherd and Martin Wolf also provided me with incisive comments and valuable advice at different stages. At GATT Mr S. K. Bagchi generously shared the benefit of his experience. To these and many others who disciplined and stimulated my thought, I am grateful. The International Centre for Economics and Related Disciplines, and the Central Research Fund of the University of London provided much-appreciated financial support. In Buenos Aires, the Centro de Economía Transnacional provided the necessary facilities for the final editing of the manuscript. I owe a very particular debt to Jorge Thomas for his moral support, as I do to Andrés Federman, Judith Evans, and Ebba Dohlman; they graciously endured endless hours of talk, sharing my hard-to-come-by insights and my all too frequent doubts. They will welcome publication of the book if only because they will no longer have to hear me talk about it. Last but not least, my work would not have been possible without the silent support of the many women to whom I was able to delegate my domestic responsibilities. Perhaps my greatest debt is to my daughters, Ximena and Natalia, for forbearance and because from them I have learnt to be patient.

Diana Tussie
July 1986

Introduction

It is in the determination of international trade policy that the gap between economic theory and practice can be seen at its widest. Those trained in conventional economics will normally look at the theory of comparative advantage and conclude that the greatest gains will be derived by applying this to national policies. Yet trade policies in most countries are continually focusing on bilateral trade imbalances and trade officials remain intent on preserving national markets. Economists have cast the blame for this dissociation between theory and practice on the short-sighted political interests of governments. Such shortsightedness was seen at its worst, it has been argued, during the 1930s when the scramble for markets led ultimately to war. With post-war reconstruction came the belief that an international institution could help to further the cause of global free trade, prosperity and peace by assisting governments to fend off protectionist demands from their constituents. It was believed that such an institution could bridge the divide between theory and practice by prodding governments to adjust their standard trade practices in order to fit the theory. Theory was left unchallenged. And so the General Agreement on Tariffs and Trade came into being. It was signed in 1947 as part of the preparatory negotiations to set up an International Trade Organization (ITO). It was intended to be merely a temporary treaty to serve until the ITO was implemented. But since the latter was never ratified, GATT by default became the basis on which successive rounds of negotiations on tariff reductions were conducted.

The ITO (and by extension the GATT) was conceived as one leg of a tripod that was to manage different areas of international economic relations: the International Monetary Fund was designed to provide short-term finance to relieve countries of the necessity to deflate or restrict imports unduly when faced with temporary balance of payments deficits; the International Bank for Reconstruction and Development to offer long-term capital assistance; and lastly, the ITO to promote freer trade and to regulate trade policies.

GATT's guiding principles reflected the prevailing liberal consensus on free trade as a generator of world prosperity and as conducive to stable peace. In the developed world, it was widely believed that the lesson of the 1930s was that peace, prosperity, and free trade, were inextricably linked. Keynes, having advocated increasing British self-sufficiency in the early 1930s, had also joined the free trade consensus by the end of the war. America took steps in the direction of a system of freer trade as early as 1934, with the Reciprocal Trade Agreements Act. Four years after the United States took the initiative with protectionism and the imposition of the Smoot–Hawley Tariff, the newly installed Roosevelt Administration changed course and initiated a series of bilateral agreements. Secretary of State Cordell Hull offered to reduce American tariffs in exchange for equivalent concessions from its trading partners. Any such reduction would be extended to other countries enjoying most favoured nation (MFN) treatment by virtue of pre-existing trade treaties. Thus, as the United States moved into a position of leadership and Great Britain's role declined, the trading order changed shape. While Britain had sustained a policy of unilateral free imports regardless of its trade deficit, the United States would seek contractual and reciprocal freeing of trade and would, moreover, be more concerned with producing a surplus on its trade account. Britain would also reform and adopt the bargaining style after the passing of the Import Duties Act of 1932; at the Conference convened at Ottawa Britain bargained with the colonies and Dominions, offering to preserve exclusive tariff-free treatment for their products in exchange for preferential access to their markets.

The GATT took up two elements of the model laid out by the United States' tariff bargaining, reciprocity and MFN treatment. In the Preamble, the contracting parties to GATT agreed to enter into 'reciprocal and mutually advantageous arrangements directed to the substantial reduction of tariffs and other barriers to trade and to the elimination of discriminatory treatment.' These two basic principles—MFN treatment and reciprocity of concessions—were further specified in Article I and Article XXVIII.

It is generally agreed that the system worked well for the developed countries (Curzon, 1965; Kock, 1969; Dam, 1970). A total of seven major negotiations have been concluded by the GATT contracting parties since 1947 and one is under way at the time of writing. There has certainly been substantial liberalization of trade in manufactures and total international trade has grown dramatically both in volume and value terms. From the early 1950s until 1980, international trade grew six times in volume. Moreover, industrial countries increased their share in the value of world exports from 65 per cent in 1950 to 80 per cent in 1970. The GATT enjoyed the confidence of many, if not most, developed countries. Its strength lay in being a 'club' of like-minded Western countries (Curzon, 1973).

The less developed countries (LDCs), on the other hand, saw their corresponding share in the value of world exports decline from 35 per cent in 1950 to 20 per cent, until the oil price shock of 1973. It became conventional wisdom that the GATT, being instrumental in the expansion of trade and the prosperity of the developed countries, had neglected the LDCs. When the first United Nations Conference on Trade and Development (UNCTAD) convened in Geneva in 1964, the rules of GATT came under attack for the exclusion of the LDCs from the benefits of post-war expansion. LDCs' objections to the rules of GATT have centred on the belief that the role envisaged for them is one of perpetuating their existence as exporters of primary commodities, while the more dynamic industrial occupations were reserved for the developed countries. The motive for this identification was the theory of comparative advantage which provided GATT's intellectual underpinning and which had traditionally been expounded in too static a framework.

The reasons for the GATT's failure in this respect were summarized by Raúl Prebisch:

> Why has GATT not been as efficacious for the developing countries as for the industrial countries? There are two main reasons. First, [it] is based on the classic concept that the free play of international economic forces by itself leads to the optimum expansion of trade and the most efficient utilisation of the world's productive resources; rules and principles are therefore established to guarantee this free play. Secondly, the rules and principles in question have not always been strictly complied with and, even though they seem to have been observed in the letter in certain instances, the spirit underlying them has not been respected. [UNCTAD *Proceedings*, 1964, Vol. II, p. 18.]

Prebisch's statement is an illustration of the tug of war in which LDCs' grievances were caught. There is first a critique of the concept of free trade, but this is no sooner stated than a condemnation of assaults to it follows. It is never clear whether the principle itself or its violation is to carry the blame. LDCs also alternated between these two contrasting positions, at times in favour of a reform of principles, at others demanding more respect for those same principles.

My objective in this study is to examine the way in which LDCs have responded and adjusted to the trading order as reflected in GATT. It suggests that the GATT can neither be blamed for the exclusion of the LDCs from the expansion of world trade in the post-war period nor take complete credit for the rapid expansion among developed countries. Both trends must be seen in the context of the structure of the world economy which GATT could not but reflect. The tariff-cutting exercises were certainly achievements that contributed to creating a climate of confidence, but not necessarily themselves the engine of trade expansion. Even within liberal thought, experts disagree as to whether trade is the engine of growth or simply an auxiliary tool, and whether a vigorous trade sector is the cause or the consequence of tariff cutting (Díaz Alejandro & Helleiner, 1983, p. 9). The 'engine' school of thought gives the credit of post-war prosperity to the tariff liberalization staged at the GATT. Previous works on the GATT can be largely ascribed to this school.

The study centres on LDCs' reactions to the GATT order; it is, therefore, concerned with manufactures rather than with primary products. There appears to be only limited choice about the location of production and direction of trade for primary products, and there has traditionally been a net flow of primary goods from the LDCs to developed countries. Precisely because of the problems connected with their reliance on primary commodities, LDCs attempted to diversify their exports.

Nine of GATT's twenty-three founding members were LDCs, but until the late 1950s the relationship beween LDCs and the GATT was a dormant one.[1] LDCs on the whole remained indifferent to the work of GATT and other GATT members on the whole remained convinced that the benefits of trade liberalization and trade expansion among the developed countries would somehow trickle down to the LDCs by virtue of the MFN clause.

The year 1958 is a turning-point in the history of GATT's relations with the LDCs. A panel comprised of Gottfried Haberler (Chairman), Roberto de Oliveira Campos, James Meade and Jan Tinbergen was appointed to examine for the first time the failure of the export trade of LDCs to expand at a rate commensurate with their import needs. This was the first major acknowledgement that the LDCs' exports faced a predicament and that this could be due 'in no small measure to the trade policies of developed countries' (Dam, 1970, p. 229), rather than to simple mismanagement or strictly domestic problems. The publication of the report gave rise to expectations in the LDCs of greater activity in the GATT to promote their trade and development needs in consonance. The number of countries showing an interest in acceding to GATT increased. Moreover, the LDCs began to join ranks and became an active pressure group from then on.

The initial stance of the LDCs *vis-à-vis* the GATT aimed at expanding their rights to free themselves from the rules of the GATT. LDCs challenged the two core principles of the GATT: equality of treatment and reciprocity of tariff concessions. Neither, they held, took into account the structural inequalities between the LDCs and the developed countries. In the words of the Indian representatives to the GATT, 'Equality of treatment is equitable only among equals. A weakling cannot carry the same load as a giant' (quoted in Kock, 1969, p. 289). This proposition became the guiding principle of the reform drive.

The thrust of the LDCs' action dealt with both the export and the import side of their tade. For the import side they demanded greater flexibility to protect their domestic markets for their infant industries. On the same grounds, they also pleaded for the removal of the obligation to grant reciprocal tariff restrictions. Regarding their exports, they lobbied for preferential tariff treatment in the markets of the developed countries. Underlying the argument for tariff preferences was also an infant industry consideration. As newcomers to the market, LDCs' infant industries could not compete with their already well-established, highly productive competitors. Without export markets, economies of scale could not be realized. A margin of preference between the tariff imposed by developed countries on the exports of old, established producers and those of LDCs could counterbalance the handicap. Chapter 2 reviews the reform of the GATT procedures to accommodate these demands. In the area of diplomacy, the LDCs attained a considerable degree of success. With the momentum gathered by the process of decolonization and their newly acquired numerical majority in the GATT, they succeeded in getting many of their demands accommodated and achieving greater room to manœuvre. Yet dissatisfaction persisted; there were obstacles still hindering the effective integration of the LDCs into the international trading system. To understand these obstacles, which mere reform of the GATT rules could not remove, it is necessary to look at the structure of world trade and the specific pattern of trade liberalization since World War II. Chapter 3 therefore puts the GATT into a wider context by highlighting the structural forces that, having allowed the expansion of trade among developed countries to proceed smoothly, could not operate for LDCs. It aims, first, to constrast both the GATT myth and LDCs' demands with the realities of world trade and, second, to provide the setting for the subsequent themes.

Both the GATT philosophy and LDCs' demands have been excessively influenced by the neo-classical theory of international trade. Based on the principle of comparative advantage, it anticipated that trade would be greater betweeen dissimilar economies than between similar ones. Yet there has been an enormous gulf between the theory and the realities of international trade. Trade flows are greater and they have grown faster between developed countries with similar economic structures than between developed and LDCs. In practice, therefore, differences in factor endowments cannot provide the whole explanation of trade. Other factors must be introduced to understand the nature and consequence of international trade.

The growth of trade is related to four intimately connected trends. Firstly, trade has been coupled with the mobility of capital to a degree unanticipated by conventional theory. While 80 per cent of world trade has been concentrated among the developed countries, so has two-thirds of international investment. Secondly, international firms have increasingly engaged in intra-industry trade (trade in products belonging to the same industrial sector), so that countries have been drawn closer together. With intra-industry trade, no country specializes completely in one or two products, and production of any single good is not concentrated in one country; national specialization not only occurs *within* a narrow segment of a given industry. It is therefore possible to retain productive activities across all industrial sectors. Thirdly, the market has become increasingly oligopolized under the direction provided by the network of international investments. Where production takes place under oligopolistic conditions, trade ceases to be essentially ruled by price competition; firms and countries largely compete on other grounds, by virtue of the technological component of industry and continuous innovation. Fourthly, some of these international firms have tended to promote an international division of labour within their own organizations so that a sizeable part of the growth of international trade is in effect the growth of such intra-firm transfers. Interlocking these four trends is the multinational corporation, which has provided an order and a dynamic infrastructure to the direction and composition of international trade flows.

The first implication of the points drawn out by Chapter 3 is that GATT's tariff-cutting role was painless in sectors and among countries where oligopolistic forms of competition prevailed. Oligopolistic production enables some concertation among producers; it also allows for supply management, so that friction may be ironed out at the production stage before it spills over onto trade. For this reason, GATT could free industrial trade far better than agricultural trade, which essentially retains price-competitive features and where the normal rules of supply and demand prevail. The technological development of agriculture has not led to intrasectorial specialization as it has done in industry. It has led instead to greater production of the same commodity at lower prices, further enhancing the price-competitive features of this market. Agriculture is an extreme case but it serves as an example. More generally, when price rules prevail the freeing of trade cannot proceed as both the GATT and neo-classical theory anticipated. If competition from foreign producers damages domestic ones, when supply cannot be managed, trade will be restrained. This has not only been applicable to the agricultural sector; it is also applicable to most industrial goods in the trade that goes both from LDCs to developed countries, and vice versa. The most tightly restrained areas of present-day international trade are those in which competition between them is felt to be most direct.

The second implication to be drawn from Chapter 3 is that South–South trade is an unlikely occurrence. The lack of mutual investment and capital mobility in this direction means that private interests have not developed the sort of links that pull developed countries together; the lack of technological specialization implies that their demand is not easily geared towards each other. They must essentially turn to the developed countries to supply them with technology. With fairly low and roughly similar labour costs, and a need to create and protect their own sources of employment, there are few immediate benefits to be found in importing low-cost labour-intensive goods from each other. Not being a natural occurrence, South–South trade requires long-term planning and large doses of political will. It must swim against the current. Not surprisingly, it has been plagued with frustrations.

The scene is now set for subsequent chapters to take a new look at the way in which LDCs have adjusted and responded to the GATT order of things and the constraints exposed in Chapter 3. LDCs' attempts to diversify their trade by promoting exports of industrial goods took two directions. On the one hand, they tried to expand industrial exports to the markets of the developed countries and, on the other, to increase trade with other LDCs (or South–South trade, as a shorthand). To take these in turn, we look first at exports of LDCs to developed countries, in Chapter 4. Here we take a sectoral approach. In the markets of developed countries, exports of textile and clothing have been the great success story. Generally, the textile industry is the first rung in the ladder of industrialization. It was central to the British Industrial Revolution, and in its labour-intensive, low technology subsectors, it is taken up, with many advantges, by countries in the process of industrialization. Given that imports of textiles and clothing are not regarded as essential to development, protection can easily be afforded to this sector, which in addition offers the twin attractions of absorbing labour and conserving foreign exchange. After successful substitution of imports, the LDCs entered the world market to use their acquired textile capacity as a foreign exchange earner. In 1976 textiles and clothing comprised more than one-third of the manufactured exports of the LDCs and exports from LDCs constituted one-fourth of world exports of textiles and clothing. While this trade is dominated by a few LDCs, most are involved in exporting textile products and many have the potential for expanding their supply capacity. This means that it is an industrial sector in which supply management is unfeasible and hence where the rules of price competition predominate. In these circumstances, LDCs' competitive goods were thought to be disrupting the markets of the importing developed countries; they were asked to restrain their exports. An elaborate system of quotas has been devised to monitor such trade.

Chapter 5 moves away from the sectoral approach and a South–North direction to take a regional approach and a South–South direction. Looking at matters in the aggregate, Keesing (1977) has shown that exports of manufactures from LDCs have mainly been absorbed by other LDCs, and Stewart (1976) showed that South–South trade mainly takes place among countries belonging to the same geographical area. Institutional arrangements have hitherto been set up among neighbouring countries. Of Latin America's total manufactured exports to other LDCs, more than 90 per cent go to other Latin American countries. In the other regions a similar, though less notable trend, is evident: in Africa 73 per cent; in the Middle East 56 per cent; and in Asia 67 per cent. This chapter concentrates on the fate of market integration efforts in Latin America. The choice of LAFTA has been motivated for three reasons. Firstly the countries of this region operate more trade with one another than in other less developed areas. Secondly, in chronological terms the Latin America Free Trade Area set up in February 1960 was the first regional integration scheme among LDCs. Thirdly, LAFTA constituted the first and the last trading arrangement among LDCs which stemmed largely from the regulations of GATT's Article XXIV. Subsequent

South–South initiatives tended, on the one hand, to deviate more from orthodox GATT prescriptions and, on the other, to benefit from some of the achievements and failures of LAFTA.

The choice of issues selected excludes a host of others which the GATT covers. The study is, therefore, not a chronicle of LDCs' activities in GATT. It aims, rather, to analyse the way in which the regulation of international trade has affected LDCs and the ways in which they have reacted to the constraints imposed by the system. Too much of the theoretical discussion on trade has been excessively concerned with deriving normative principles. Too often, assumptions about the trade policies of other countries have been absent. Economists are sometimes inclined to scorn governments which have mercantilist trade policies instead of enjoying the gains from freer trade. Because of the normative bias, a bundle of accepted conventional theories about the functioning of the international trading system has too often gone untested by pragmatic study. The main purpose of this book is to interpret recent tendencies in the world trading system and to reinterpret past ones inspired by the thought that:

> History for [a scholar] is not just an optional subject, something that historians do. It is not just a vital, passionate quality of the thought that makes the data of his science. History is the place he inhabits in his search for pattern, regularity, order, principle. It is the world itself. [Donelan, 1978, p. 14.]

NOTES

1. The question of grouping and defining countries involves a number of political, economic and methodological problems which would merit a study of their own. The General Agreement in its Part IV, introduced in 1964, as we shall see, makes a clear distinction between developed and less developed countries but no criterion is given as to whether a country should be recognized as developed or less developed. The problem of definition has been obviated, if not solved, by leaving countries the freedom to decide for themselves whether they consider their economies to be less developed or not. When Part IV was introduced, Greece, Portugal, Spain and Turkey claimed less developed status in the GATT for the purpose of negotiations. This is in contrast to their position in other organizations—UNCTAD, for instance.

1 The origins of the GATT

1.1 THE BACKGROUND

The post-war economic order was built on the foundations bequeathed by the 1930s after the collapse of the gold standard and the hegemonic role of Great Britain. The 1930s had revealed beyond doubt the new weight of the United States in the world economy. In 1929 nearly 45 per cent of the world's production of manufactures was concentrated in the United States; her exports represented 20 per cent of the world's exports. Nevertheless, such a substantial share of world exports was not an important part of American income: it represented only 6 per cent of its GNP. The United States was much more self-sufficient than Britain had ever been. Pre-war British exports comprised 16 per cent of world exports, but they had contributed a share of 20 per cent to British GNP. Although American imports comprised 12.5 per cent of world imports, these were again quite marginal for the functioning of the American economy because of its sheer size and the uniqueness of its natural resource base (Kenwood & Lougheed, 1983).[1]

When the Depression set in, the United States Congress enacted the Smoot–Hawley tariff, which increased the protection afforded to the domestic market on nine hundred items. Britain, faced with an unmanageable trade deficit, abandoned the gold standard in 1931 and ended its century of free trade in 1932 with the passing of the Import Duties Act. As other countries moved in self-defence to restrict their imports, adopting 'beggar-my-neighbour' measures, a downward spiral in international trade was set in motion. By the end of 1932 the volume of trade in manufactures had declined by 40 per cent (Lewis, 1949, p. 50).

With the Democratic victory in the United States presidential elections of 1932, a new conception of America's role in the world began to take shape. It was Secretary of State Cordell Hull's belief that the United States had to take the initiative to arrest the protectionist wave. He was convinced that the elimination of trade barriers was the principal means of halting the downward spiral in international trade, to achieve a stable, prosperous world economy and thereby reduce political tensions. As he put it: 'enduring peace and the welfare of nations are indissolubly connected with friendliness, fairness, equality and the maximum practicable degree of freedom in international trade.' (in Dam, 1970, p. 12). He further believed that:

> unhampered trade dovetailed with peace; high tariffs, trade barriers, and unfair economic competition, with war . . . if we could get a freer flow of trade . . . so that one country would not be deadly jealous of another and the living standards of all countries might rise, thereby eliminating the economic dissatisfaction that breeds war, we might have a reasonable chance of lasting peace [in Gardner, 1969, p. 9].

Cordell Hull actively lobbied Congress and managed to get approval for an amendment of the Smoot–Hawley 1930 Act, the Reciprocal Trade Agreements Act of 1934. The new Act empowered the President, for a period of three years, to initiate trade agreements on the basis of reciprocal reductions in duties. In the period up to the outbreak of World War II, the United States concluded reciprocal agreements with twenty-nine countries on the basis of most favoured nation treatment. The impact on tariffs was small but the procedure stamped a mark of origin on to the post-war trading rules.[2]

As the war drew to an end, with the United States holding a substantial trade surplus with the rest of the world, a considerable body of opinion argued that the quid pro quo approach was a misconception. The substantial balance of payments surplus warranted unilateral reductions on the part of the United States so that, with the opening-up of her market to other countries' exports, the gap between deficits and surpluses could be bridged. Professor Hubert D. Henderson, advising the British Government argued that:

> The principle of reciprocal concessions comes very near to saying that tariff reductions, calculated to increase American imports, can only be made in return for tariff concessions by other countries, calculated to increase American exports by an equivalent amount. This, in turn, comes very near to making it a *sine qua non* of tariff reductions that they should do nothing to . . . readjust the balance of payments of the world. [Henderson, 1949, pp. 611–12.]

In order to secure a balanced international economy, he recommended that countries reduce their tariffs and encourage imports, not in proportion to the reciprocal concessions they are able to secure, but in proportion to the strength of their balance of payments position.

The recommendation bore affinities to Keynes' International Clearing Union by which countries in surplus would be required to increase their imports to ease the adjustment of deficit countries. As Henderson himself acknowledged, this was far removed from 'the reign of acceptability' to American public opinion.

The quid pro quo approach was institutionalized in GATT. The uniqueness of the United States' resource base and its variegated economy meant that strong producer interests could be found in favour both of protection and of free trade. Its foreign trade policy had of necessity to balance out political pressures and counter-pressures on the home front. Its adoption of a liberal trade policy was less ambiguous, less across-the-board than Britain's had ever been. As noted by F. V. Meyer (1978), the major difference between the trading order under the *Pax Britannica* and that under the *Pax Americana* was that Britain had reduced tariffs unilaterally and sustained not only a free export policy, but a free import policy also. In contrast, the United States offered to free its imports on a contractual basis, with an eye to reciprocal benefits at the conclusion of negotiations, regardless of handicaps at the starting line.[3]

1.2. POST-WAR PLANNING AND THE GATT

Soon after the entry of the United States into the war, talks were started between the United States—the sunrise power—and Britain—the sunset power—on trade and monetary collaboration to be conducted after the war.

The Keynesian revolution had led to an acceptance at the national level that market forces were not automatically self-regulating and that a certain form of government intervention was therefore required from time to time. Concurrently, at the international level, it was also conceded that government management was necessary; and disagreement was confined to the extent of such intervention. It was widely accepted by both sides that the collapse of the 1930s was largely due to the lack of international consultative mechanisms that had left economic affairs at the mercy of unregulated market forces.

The aim of the Bretton Woods agreements was to re-establish by international agreement 'a reasonable facsimile of the gold standard system' (Stolper, 1949, p. 260), i.e., the conditions for an international system which would secure the combination of currency convertibility, capital mobility and free trade. Three major institutions—the International Monetary Fund, the International Bank for Reconstruction and Development and the International Trade Organization—were planned to achieve this objective. They were also given powers of multilateral surveillance to ensure that rules were not capriciously breached. It was thought that with multilateral surveillance a re-enactment of the collapse of the 1930s could be averted.

The first two institutions were created as a result of the conference held at Bretton Woods in 1944. At Bretton Woods the signatories undertook to maintain the inter-convertibility of their currencies, to refrain from competitive devaluations and from bilateral currency arrangements which would discriminate among trading partners in current transactions. The appropriate financial arrangements were thus laid out for multilateal trade and free exchange to develop. Commercial policy, however, was not directly involved and negotiations on this particular issue went much more slowly. There were two reasons for this. There were differences in British and American views as well as different views within each government. In the United States the more ardent free-traders in the Department of State, inspired by Cordell Hull's global vision, confronted sectoral interests in the Department of Agriculture as well as in Congress.

Negotiations for the International Trade Organization (ITO) began in 1946. Successive conferences took place from 1946 to 1948 in London, New York, Geneva and Havana. The final version of the ITO charter was drawn up in Havana in March 1948 but it never came into effect. The initial proposal for the ITO had been largely conceived by Department of State officials but, anticipating a strong rebuff, President Truman never submitted it to Congress for ratification (US Department of State, 1945 and 1946). In fact only two countries, Australia and Liberia, ever ratified it.

In 1947 President Truman was determined to use his Congressional power to negotiate tariff reductions under the Reciprocal Trade Agreements Act, which had been renewed in 1945 for a period of three years. This law authorized the President to reduce import duties by up to 50 per cent in return for equivalent concessions by other countries. The Administration proposed to negotiate such trade agreements simultaneously and to embody them in one multilateral treaty. Thus, the General Agreement on Tariffs and Trade was drawn up as the general framework of rights and obligations for the twenty-two countries—of which nine were LDCs—participating in the tariff negotiations sponsored by the United States. The GATT came into being before the Havana Conference, but in accordance with the draft Charter for ITO that was currently being discussed. It was originally envisaged as the first of a number of agreements that were to be negotiated under the auspices of ITO. When it became clear that the Havana Charter would not be ratified by the United States, the General Agreement became by default the under-pinning of an international institution. Thus, GATT is not technically an organization of which countries become members but a treaty with con-tracting parties. Nevertheless, it has assumed the commercial policy role that had been planned for ITO, without incorporating the wider provisions of the Havana Charter on restrictive business practices, commodity agreements, economic development and full employment policies. It mainly deals, in contrast, with the reduction of tariffs on trade in manufactures.

1.3   THE GATT'S OPERATIONAL STRUCTURE

In discussing the basic principles and mechanisms of the GATT, we must consider two interrelated levels. In the first instance, the GATT brings together a body of principles. It is an international, contractual agreement by which each signatory or contracting party commits itself to treat all other signatories according to the most favoured nation (MFN) standard. In the second instance, the GATT is a forum where countries negotiate tariff reductions according to the legal framework provided by the agreement.

In GATT member countries are not required to abolish tariffs automatically. Rather, tariffs are the negotiable item: countries make specific agreements to reduce particular tariffs in exchange for a reciprocal reduction from a trading partner. In the absence of such an agreement a contracting party is not obliged to make a reduction.[4]

The Preamble to the General Agreement presents the goals of the contracting parties:

> that their relations in the field of trade and economic endeavour should be conducted with a view to raising standards of living, ensuring full employment and a large and steadily growing volume of real income and effective demand, developing the full use of the resources of the world and expanding the production and exchange of goods, [and]
>
> to contribute to these objectives by entering into reciprocal and mutually advantageous arrangements directed to the substantial reduction of tariffs and other barriers to trade, and to the elimination of discriminatory treatment in international commerce.

The key principle of the General Agreement is the MFN clause contained in Article I. This imposes on the contracting parties the obligation to grant each other equality of treatment:

> any advantage, favour, privilege or immunity granted by any contracting party to any product originating in or destined for any other country shall be accorded immediately and unconditionally to the like product originating in or destined for the territories of all other contracting parties.

The clause was specifically designed to outlaw preferential arrangements and, as a corollary, to prevent the struggle to obtain and secure such arrangements. The widespread use of discriminatory trade and currency arrangements was believed to have contributed to the political tension of the 1930s and ultimately to war. The GATT expressed the belief that a liberal trading system would convert competition for the control of territories into price competition. If every country undertook to apply the same tariff to all its foreign suppliers, competition for markets would be open and confined to prices; it would therefore contribute to economic efficiency rather than lead to economic warfare. Many of the founders and intellectual begetters of the postwar economic order believed there was a link between free trade and the possibility of international peace. As we have seen, one of those who saw such a security link was Cordell Hull, US Secretary of State from 1933 to 1944. His vision lingered on and continued to be influential in the Department of State for many years after his period of office.

Besides regulating competition in the international market, the GATT also aimed to regulate the method by which a country could protect its domestic producers from such competition. In theory, countries were supposed to have no other form of protection but tariffs. Being the sole legal device, tariffs are also, in principle, the sole negotiable item in the GATT. Protection through non-tariff measures (NTMs),[5] such as import quotas, was to be banned. No provision was therefore made for negotiations to reduce NTMs. The text of the General Agreement contains very vague provisions with respect to the use of NTMs and only in relation to balance of payments problems and non-industrial goods (agricultural production and fisheries).

In its original form, the GATT agreement consisted of three parts:

Part I obliges all parties to grant general MFN treatment to each other; enshrines the principles of non-discrimination; and enumerates the exceptions.

Part II contains policy rules dealing with transit trade, anti-dumping duties, subsidies, quantitative restrictions, state enterprises, etc. Its provisions are binding in so far as they do not conflict with state legislation. Hence, a country may accede to GATT provisionally without complete acceptance of Part II.

Part III contains institutional rules for tariff negotiations, accession and withdrawal of countries, conditions of application of the Agreement as well as the safeguard provisions to which countries can resort in exceptional circumstances.

A new class of provisions was added in 1964 to incorporate some of the innovations that LDCs had lobbied for. These provisions were brought together under Part IV. The core provision of this part was that LDCs would no longer be required to offer reciprocity in tariff negotiations.

In contrast to the IMF and the World Bank where a system of weighted voting operates, in GATT each country is entitled to one vote. Voting rules vary according to the subject under discussion. An amendment to Part I (containing the obligation to grant MFN treatment) and to Articles XIX (safeguard action in imports) and XXX (amendments) can only be passed if it is unanimously agreed upon. Amendments to the other parts become effective once they have been accepted by a two-thirds majority, but are only effective among those who have agreed to them. This highlights the contractual rather than mandatory role of GATT. Equally, a two-thirds majority is required to grant a waiver to a government wanting to take measures that are incompatible with its obligations, for example an import surcharge. All other decisions are taken by a majority of votes cast (Article XXV).

The GATT's main business consists in the arrangement of the periodical conferences or 'rounds' at which the members bargain for mutual concessions. In the early stages there were no provisions for secretariat services; the secretariat was provided by the Interim Commission for the ITO, which, after the *de facto* rejection of the Havana Charter, was made available to GATT by the United Nations in 1952. A Committee for Agenda and International Business was formed in 1951 to exercise surveillance functions. This Committee was replaced in 1960 by a Council of Representatives with broader decision-making powers. The Council of Representatives holds regular sessions concerned with the granting of waivers, the application of the GATT's rules, accession of new members and general trade policy issues.

The accession of new members requires the agreement of a two-thirds majority vote. No one country can exercise the power of veto. Majority rule was preferred over unanimity to obviate a situation in which the accession of a country might be impeded by a member with little interest in its market or by a country competing with it. However, member countries which have not assented to the accession of a particular country are not obliged to apply the provisions of the Agreement *vis-à-vis* the new member (Article XXXV). In other words, membership does not automatically force a country to grant equal treatment to all participating countries, although this is the desired end result. Here is another instance of the contractual character of GATT. Article XXXV was used most extensively at the time of Japanese accession in 1955. To retain their restrictions on imports from Japan, fourteen countries invoked Article XXXV (Dam, 1970, pp. 347–50). The Japanese experience is closely connected with the regulation of textile exports and the history of a polemical notion in world trade 'market disruption', as we shall see in subsequent chapters.

Altogether, these provisions aimed to establish as open and liberal a system as possible that would allow trade to increase global efficiency. The GATT aimed to codify a system which was thought to be more realistic than absolute free trade. The drafters and the founding members considered absolute free trade the first best policy but acknowledged that it would not be politically feasible to enforce it at all times regardless of domestic employment levels. The GATT was regarded as a pragmatic compromise, a 'second best', by which domestic interests were offered some protection from the international market, but foreign suppliers would be allowed to compete for a share of the domestic market. With the creation of an appropriate institution, there would, moreover, be a framework for collective discipline. With such collective rules it was hoped that the international trading system would be strengthened in order to avoid strains similar to those of the 1930s which resulted from the scramble for self-protection. The GATT adopted the traditional MFN principle of non-discrimination with two innovations. The first innovation is that negotiations for tariff reductions in GATT take place simultaneously. The second innovation is the safeguarding of these reductions against future rises. While Article I ensures that tariff concessions are to be extended to all contracting parties, Article II provides future stability for these concessions. The agreed rates are 'bound' and put together in 'schedules' for each country. Once 'bound', these rates can only be raised after renegotiation with the country holding the 'initial negotiating rights' (Article XXVIII), that is, the country that had bargained and 'paid' for the concession in the first place, as well as with those that might have become the principal supplying countries since that time. Concessions thereby become the collective right of the contracting parties to GATT, regardless of which country has negotiated them. A contracting party that wishes to raise a bound tariff must be prepared to offer compensation or risk retaliation (Article XIX). Given that legally bound tariffs are an integral part of the General Agreement, a newcomer automatically benefits from the cumulative effect of all concessions negotiated prior to its arrival (since, on accession, it is entitled to MFN treatment). The newcomer is therefore expected to pay an 'entry fee' on accession: it must enter into tariff negotiations with established contracting parties before becoming a full member. The general thrust of activities in GATT is to maintain a balance of concessions.

To ensure that all foreign suppliers should stand on an equal footing in their competition for a part of the domestic market, the General Agreement only accepted the tariff as a legitimate device for safeguarding the domestic market. There was yet a second reason for the legitimacy of the tariff as opposed to quantitative restrictions:

> In the minds of those who have done most to initiate and to push forward the project (of the GATT), a strong dislike of quantitative regulation, as something inconsistent with, and inimical to, a self-adjusting price system, has played throughout a prominent part. [Henderson, 1949, p. 613.]

On the grounds that quantitative restrictions allow discrimination among foreign exporters and, by predetermining the volume of trade, alter the 'correct' price relations, quantitative restrictions on trade were prohibited. In principle, they could only be applied in strictly limited, carefully defined circumstances.

A further provision was designed to ensure non-discrimination. Once foreign goods passed the frontier, they would be ensured equal rights of competition with domestic goods. They were to be given 'national treatment' (as defined in Article III), i.e. they would not be subject to measures of a discriminatory nature, such as higher taxes, *vis-à-vis* those produced domestically.

The major trading countries were successful in putting these provisions into practice. Trade liberalization among them was accomplished through removal of quantitative restrictions as convertibility of their currencies was restored and through a series of multilateral trade negotiations in GATT. The

GATT has sponsored seven 'rounds' of negotiations following the pace set by United States' trade legislation. The first five rounds of negotiations (Geneva, 1947; Annecy, 1949; Torquay, 1950–51; Geneva, 1956; Dillon Round in Geneva, 1960–62) corresponded to successive renewals of the Reciprocal Trade Agreements Act of 1934. The Kennedy Round which began in 1964 was the international counterpart of the Trade Expansion Act of 1962; the Tokyo Round which began in 1973 was rendered possible by the 1974 Trade Act. At the time of writing, the United States is spearheading a drive to negotiate trade liberalization in the service sector under the aegis of the GATT. 'The GATT is (largely) the international counterpart of US tariff policy' (Meyer, 1978, p. 126).

These rounds of negotiations have concentrated primarily on tariff reductions, but gradually broader issues concerning the problems of LDCs and non-tariff measures have increasingly come to the fore. During the Tokyo Round, a whole series of codes on non-tariff matters were negotiated and concluded, apart from the tariff reductions and the improvement of some elements of the General Agreement in favour of LDCs.

The average tariff rate of industrialized countries on industrial products will be 6.5 per cent when the final Tokyo Round reductions come into effect. The largest tariff reductions have been made in engineering goods (GATT, 1979), especially in machinery and transport, which is also the sector that has grown fastest (Table 3.4). The results of these multilateral rounds can be summarized as follows: low levels of MFN tariff rates, at least in the developed countries and with respect to most non-agricultural products, together with the removal of quantitative restrictions in a large number of these sectors; a series of codes governing the use of certain non-tariff measures (accepted mainly by the developed countries so far); and the consolidation of the position of the GATT as the prime forum for the discussion of trade policy issues and the settlement of disputes.

1.4 THE GATT'S PROVISIONS FOR THE LDCS

The original text of the General Agreement gave no explicit recognition to the special trade problems of underdeveloped countries. Orthodoxy had admitted that reasonable security of employment could not be guaranteed by the play of unregulated market forces, but this reformulation of *laissez-faire* was not extended to international trade. So far as relations between countries were concerned, the neo-classical belief was that growth in itself would bring the correction of disparities through the free play of market forces.

The most violent controversies at Havana and the most protracted ones were those evoked by issues raised in the name of economic development.

> . . . The underdeveloped countries attacked the draft at several points. . . .
> They sought freedom to set up new preferential systems, impose import
> quotas, and employ other restrictive devices without prior approval. And
> they proposed that a semi-autonomous economic development committee
> be established within the trade organisation for the purpose of facilitating
> these escapes. [Wilcox, 1949, pp. 48–9.][6]

While largely unsuccessful, the underdeveloped countries did achieve the
inclusion of a chapter dealing with development as part of the problem of
post-war reconstruction included in the Havana Charter, the thrust of which
was reflected in GATT's Article XVIII. Article XVIII recognized that:

> special governmental assistance may be required to promote the estab-
> lishment, development or reconstruction of particular industries or
> branches of agriculture, and that in appropriate circumstances the grant of
> such assistance in the form of protective measures is justified

The provisions permitted a country to deviate from the general provisions on
bound tariff concessions or the prohibition on quantitative restrictions when
this was necessary to pursue their development objectives, notably for the
establishment of infant industries or to protect their balance of payments.
Actions of this nature were to be subject to multilateral surveillance and
approval, and countries invoking Article XVIII were still subject to the
obligation not to tilt the given balance of concessions. They faced requests for
compensation or the threat of retaliation from other countries that considered
that their interests were injured. The applicant had to prove that its proposed
import restriction

> is necessary . . . in order to achieve, a fuller or more economic use of [its]
> natural resources and manpower and, in the long run, to raise the standard
> of living within [its] territory . . . and is unlikely to have a harmful effect, in
> the long run, on international trade.

The escape hatch provided by this Article could equally be applied by
countries engaged in economic development or post-war reconstruction.
Because of the GATT's devotion to the principle of non-discrimination, there
was as yet no awareness of problems relating to particular categories of
countries or particular types of trade. As far as underdeveloped countries were
concerned, however, 'Art. XVIII reflected the predominance of the import
substitution approach to economic development.' (Dam, 1970, p. 227). In a
review session carried out in 1954–5, references to reconstruction were
dropped, and LDCs' rights to resort to protection were laid out more clearly.
The Article overall was a reflection of the industrialization policy that was
already being followed by the old-established LDCs and by the newly-
established countries that were in the process of acquiring independence,
such as India, Pakistan, Ceylon, Indonesia, Phillipines, Burma and that had

participated at Havana in their own right. Their industrialization policies were no more than a deliberate attempt to continue practices acquired since the Depression and to protect their war-boosted industries from unrestrained competition, mainly with the booming American industrial sector. At the preparatory session for the Havana Conference held in London, India voiced the thought that domestic planning for industrialization required the planning of foreign trade as well, in order to increase exports and restrict imports to essentials. A country like India therefore claimed freedom in the field of tariffs, quantitative restriction and subsidies (Kock, 1969, p. 225).

Until the end of the 1950s there is no evidence that attention was devoted to the need to provide special stimuli for the exports of LDCs. Whether members of GATT or not, LDCs had a defensive attitude; they took what Dam has defined as 'the passive legislative approach to trade problems which was typical of the early GATT' (p. 227). They concentrated their efforts on preserving freedom of action to insulate their domestic markets from import competition. The following chapter will trace the later change in attitudes and the reforms achieved.

NOTES

1. In 1954 imports comprised a mere 1 per cent of GNP. Since then they have increased gradually: in 1964 they comprised 2 per cent of GNP, in 1974 6 per cent and in 1984 9 per cent.
2. In fact Britain had also converted to negotiating on tariffs at Ottawa in 1932, two years before the Reciprocal Trade Agreements Act. It could be argued that this is GATT's first antecedent. Britain, however, did not institute reciprocity in negotiations, nor extend the result of the negotiations to non-Commonwealth countries on an MFN basis. Both of these principles became bones of contention between the United States and Britain during the subsequent post-war discussions.
3. Reciprocity surfaced in new clothing in 1982 when Senator Danforth, with an eye to the deficit with Japan, made a move to demand reciprocity in bilateral balances, country-by-country and sector-by-sector.
4. The twentieth-century history of commercial policy offers few examples of unrequested, unilateral tariff reductions: in 1950 West Germany cut tariffs in order to arrest inflationary pressures; in Latin America Chile, Argentina, Uruguay and Peru did likewise in the mid-1970s; in 1969 and 1983–86 Japan unilaterally undertook some liberalization, though pressure had been exerted on her because of her large trade surplus.
5. The term 'tariff measures' rather than the more commonplace 'tariff barriers' has been deliberately used in the text. The term 'barrier' may be seen to imply that a natural flow of a certain element—in this case, trade—is being interrupted or restricted. Thus, the implicit assumption behind the term 'barrier' is that free trade is the natural state of things. The term 'tariff measure' may be equally value-laden, but it avoids that particular connotation.
6. The author took part in the Havana Conference as Vice-Chairman of the American delegation.

2 The reform of the GATT

2.1 THE BATTLE OF IDEAS

The classical Ricardian trade theory of comparative advantage and its reformulated version into the Hecksher–Ohlin–Samuelson theory held full sway when the Bretton Woods agreements were signed and the establishment of an International Trade Organization was debated in 1945–8. It was an accepted doctrine that each country should specialize in and export those commodities which it could produce more cheaply, in exchange for those that could be produced comparatively more cheaply elsewhere. Trade would allow an efficient and profitable use of domestic factors of production; it would increase national as well as global efficiency and prosperity.[1] Trade theory was then essentially interested in drawing normative principles and relatively less concerned with the evidence of actual trade flows.

LDCs were aware that indiscriminate import liberalization would mean an end to their war-protected industrial development. New industries had boomed during the war but they would be at a disadvantage in competition with the more efficient, mature industries of the United States and Western Europe. Protection from foreign competition, it was argued, was necessary in the initial stage to allow the domestic producer to attain optimum size. But the argument did not go any further; once the infant industry reached a sufficient size, the temporary protection from external competition would be removed, and freer trade would be resumed. This view did not fundamentally challenge the foundations of the classical theory; the infant industry argument for protection is not alien to that theory. To quote from John Stuart Mill:

> The only case in which, on mere principles of political economy, protecting duties can be defensible, is when they are imposed temporarily (especially in a young and rising nation) in hopes of naturalizing a foreign industry, in itself perfectly suitable to the circumstances of the country. The superiority of one country over another in a branch of production often arises only from having begun it sooner. . . . But it cannot be expected that individuals should, at their own risk, or rather to their certain loss, introduce a new manufacture, and bear the burden of carrying it on until the producers

have been educated up to the level of those with whom the processes are traditional. A protecting duty, continued, for a reasonable time, might sometimes be the least inconvenient mode in which the nation can tax itself for the support of such an experiment [*Principles of Political Economy*, 1848, Book V, Chap. 10.]

In the very early 1950s two parallel and similar challenges were made to the free-trade doctrine from development economists. The Economic Commission for Latin America (ECLA) under the leadership of its Executive Secretary, Raúl Prebisch, put forward the argument that there were 'structural' forces in international trade which impeded the development of countries specializing in the production and export of primary commodities. There was a long-term secular decline in the terms of trade of products; therefore, trade in these products could not function as an engine of growth.[2] Simultaneously, Hans Singer, though as yet unaware of this work, presented a paper at the annual conference of the American Economic Association, with similar conclusions.[3]

In place of the smooth and equitable functioning of comparative advantage— in which each country was supposed to benefit by maximizing production of the commodities which it produced most efficiently in relation to other commodities which it could import—Singer and Prebisch found a structural bias against the producers of primary commodities. The argument focused on a secular trend to inequalities between the centre of the trading system, consisting of the developed capitalist economies, and the dependent periphery, consisting in turn of the underdeveloped countries that had specialized in the production and export of primary commodities. Such structural inequalities were reflected in the deterioration of the terms of trade between the two groups of countries. This deterioration was coupled with a slow growth of the international demand for primary commodities and resulted in a 'trade gap', i.e. a persistent tendency towards disequilibrium in the trade balance of countries relying primarily on commodity exports. As a result they lacked the resources necessary to import, on an adequate scale, the goods required for development.

This is not the place to judge the merits of this view; it has attracted a good deal of attention and has been considered to be a brilliant finding by some, an inexcusable distortion of reality by others. Irrespective of whether the terms of trade of commodities do in fact tend to deteriorate or not, this theorizing altered the conventional image of international trade. The Prebisch–Singer thesis played an important role in drawing attention to a certain link between the structure of international trade and development. Their work formed the foundation stone of what became known as the 'structuralist school'. At this stage structuralists thought of 'industrialization as the great saviour, as the escape from the dependence of the primary producer into true development as a producer of manufactured products'. (Singer, 1978, p. 58.)

In a recent review of the evolution of his own thinking, Prebisch pointed out that to a large extent the industrialization policy advocated 'sought to provide theoretical justification for the industrialization policy already being followed (especially by the large countries of Latin America), to encourage the others to follow it too, and to provide all of them with an orderly strategy for carrying this out' (Prebisch, 1982, p. 6).

The policy proposal as summarized by Prebisch is worth quoting in full for the purposes of our further discussion:

> No emphasis was put at this stage on exports of manufactures to the centres, due to the prevailing unfavourable conditions in the latter and the lack of a suitable industrial infrastructure for this. In order to spark off the beginning of this process I strongly recommended the stimulation of exports of manufactures—as well as primary goods—between Latin American countries. I envisaged preferential arrangements by regions or subregions leading in the course of time to a common market. [Prebisch, 1982, p. 8.]

The drive to export to developed countries would come as a second stage.

It is important to note that, notwithstanding their different approaches, both the structural school and the neo-classical school underpinning the GATT agree on the central importance of trade for economic development. Trade was the dynamic element in the post-war economic recovery of the European countries; it was regarded as the reliable engine of economic growth and 'had acquired an almost sacrosanct quality'. (Shonfield, 1976, p. 49). Structuralists equally believed that trade ought to be the engine of growth of LDCs. They were merely advocating a recasting of the principles of international trade in a Keynesian light. Unregulated market forces could not be relied on to solve inequalities *between* countries, just as they could not do it *within* countries.

Positive measures were required to take the international market beyond equality in legal terms to a greater mesure of equality in economic terms. As the LDCs converted to this affirmative stance, the trading system—and its management by the GATT—became the centre of the controversy. By the end of the 1950s the international debate on development was putting more and more emphasis on the expansion of industrial exports as an alternative to aid: expansion of these exports meant a quest for access to the markets of developed countries. LDCs now looked at the export side.

2.2 THE ISSUES IN THE GATT[4]

The LDCs claimed that their export interests in GATT lagged, owing to a complex of factors. Despite the fact that the General Agreement made no formal distinction in its tariff reduction rules between manufactured goods and primary commodities, one large sector of commodities, agriculture, remained protected in Europe and the United States, for strategic, political and social reasons. Moreover, in 1955 the United States sought a waiver from GATT rules in order to protect its extensive farm programme with import quotas. The United States secured 'a waiver that was exceptionally broad', bearing no time limit and requiring only an annual report (Dam, 1970, p. 260).[5] Since the United States was the largest producer and exporter of foodstuffs, the waiver in effect, disqualified the GATT for the supervision of trade in these products; their inclusion in the broad GATT aspiration to free trade became even more nominal. Finally, when the Treaty of Rome was drawn and the Common Agricultural Policy came into being it became even clearer that hopes for an unrestricted international market in agricultural products were unrealistic. Not only the export interests of the LDCs were affected, but also those of countries such as Denmark, New Zealand and Australia.

As for trade in other primary commodities, although when the Havana Charter had been discussed in 1947–8[6] there had been some recognition that this needed to be regulated, the General Agreement merely stated that its contracting parties were not prevented from joining inter-governmental commodity agreements (Article XX).

The mechanics of the tariff conferences were also blamed for excluding LDCs. Let us examine the arguments. The tariff reduction procedure rests on the assumption that access to a market is a gain that must be earned and a price that must be paid on a quid pro quo basis. This, as we have seen in the preceding chapter, was regarded as a pragmatic approach to trade liberalization, a 'second best' in which domestic interests would be assured of a certain margin of protection from foreign competition. Moreover, step-by-step negotiations on tariffs would ease the process of accommodation to foreign competition. Stemming from the regard for a quid pro quo approach, three basic rules govern tariff negotiations: the principle of reciprocity, the principal supplier rule, and MFN treatment among all contracting parties, or multilateralization to all member countries of tariff reductions obtained on a country-to-country basis.

According to the principle of reciprocity, a country will only offer tariff reductions in exchange for an equivalent concession from a trading partner. The exact meaning of reciprocity is nowhere defined in the text of the General Agreement, but none the less 'it is one of the most vital concepts in GATT practice' (Dam, 1970, p. 50). Therefore, when a country requests a tariff reduction it must be prepared to grant an equivalent concession on another item in exchange. A bargain can hence only be struck among those who have something to offer.

The customary method of measuring reciprocity is based on the concept of trade coverage, i.e. the annual volume of imports to which the tariff reduction will be applied. Percentages of tariff reduction are dismissed, as are the relative importance of a given concession to the overall economy and trade flows of the negotiating countries.

As a consequence of the requirement to grant reciprocity, and, moreover, of the way it is measured, the LDCs found that they could not request a tariff reduction because they could not offer a bargain. There were cases in which the domestic market, from the start, was not significantly protected (e.g. small countries like Barbados, Uruguay, etc.) and the room for tariff reduction was therefore limited. On the other hand, countries in the early stages of industrialization argued that they could not reduce tariffs before they achieved a good competitive position. The liberalization of trade could otherwise threaten infant industries.

Above all, for the concept of a tariff bargain to have any meaning, there must exist in the very first place an integrated and variegated economy with a healthy balance of payments with room for manœuvre to determine the volume and composition of imports. Otherwise, the volume of imports is determined primarily by the availability of foreign exchange; and the composition, by the stage of development of the economy. So the insistence of the developed countries on reciprocity in trade concessions was seen to be detrimental to the LDCs' growth. An increase in exports to developed countries as a result of a concession automatically brought with it an element of reciprocity since, given the propensities involved, that increase in LDCs' exports to developed countries was followed by a corresponding expansion in LDCs' imports from them (Prebisch, 1982). LDCs, unlike capital surplus countries, would not do other with their foreign exchange earnings than spend them on goods from the developed countries, thus making trade flows reciprocal even if tariff cuts or trade coverage were not.

The second feature of GATT tariff negotiations is the so-called principal supplier rule. By virtue of this rule, negotiations are begun bilaterally, by requests and not by offers. Requests for tariff reduction on a particular product were normally to be made by—and only by—the exporter of the largest volume of that product to the market of a second country. Not usually being in this position and, therefore, not able to request reductions, the most LDCs could hope for was that the developed countries would negotiate concessions among themselves which would include products of interest to them. Then, on the basis of the MFN clause, which comes into play at the last stage of the tariff reduction process, they would benefit from its 'splashing effect'.

The last stage of the negotiation is the truly multilateral one: once a country agrees to reduce a certain tariff, the level obtained is generalized to all the other contracting parties to GATT and bound at that level. The 'binding' of customs duties on the particular items that enter the negotiations and on which agreement is obtained is a basic concept within GATT. A given rate of customs duty on a particular item is 'bound' when an agreement has been reached with respect to it. This means that any raising of a tariff at a later date is subject to negotiation within GATT and the affected trading partners can claim compensation.

Thus, every country, in principle, will apply the same tariff to all its foreign suppliers, with just a few exceptions (customs unions, free trade areas and advantages which are granted to adjacent countries with the purpose of facilitating frontier traffic). It is at this point, when tariff reductions are extended to all members, that countries unable to participate more actively hope to benefit. Presumably, this has been one of the incentives for such countries to apply for membership of GATT and to remain within the system.

However, the 'splashing effect' of MFN treatment was found to be a double-edged sword. It precluded the LDCs from negotiating concessions among themselves: the fact that bilateral concessions, once agreed upon, had to be generalized to all countries made it impractical. Multilateralization meant that concessions could only be granted with an eye to the strongest trading powers; all tariff reductions had to keep in view the competitiveness and the capacity of these to overflow their domestic markets (Linder, 1964, p. 527).

Secondly, by virtue of the MFN principle, all countries were supposed to receive equal tariff treatment in spite of the fact that some were in a disadvantageous position in terms of competitiveness and bargaining power in the international market. The fact that all countries were to be treated equally was seen as reinforcing the imbalance in the structure of world trade. In 1955, when the contracting parties to GATT met for a review session, the Indian representative noted that 'equality of treatment is equitable only among equals'. GATT had been built to guarantee non-discrimination in world trade, but in practice it could not prevent discrimination against the weakest members unable to compete on an equal footing.

2.3 THE REFORM

Two parallel evolutions took place in the GATT with respect to LDCs after the mid-1950s. On the one hand, as in other international organizations, membership from this group of countries increased—mainly because of the independence of new states. Article XXVI provides that if a colonial power had previously accepted the General Agreement with respect to its colonies, when independence was obtained, the new state should be deemed to be a contracting party. A system was established by which such former colonies became *de facto* members pending final decisions as to their commercial policy. *De facto* membership means that although such countries do not fully apply GATT trading rules, they have a right to participate in its meetings and to vote. A large majority of these new states, having more pressing problems to solve than participation in GATT, confined themselves to following the moves of older, more experienced and active peers, such as Brazil, Chile and India. None the less, however passive the newer states were, they provided these older LDC members with a supportive constituency for their aim of obtaining a more favourable deal in the GATT system. The first comprehensive study of the operation of GATT with respect to the exports of LDCs appeared in 1958. This report may be considered a turning-point in the history of LDCs in the GATT. It was carried out by a panel of renowned economists, one of whom was Brazilian—Roberto Campos. The others were James Meade, Jan Tinbergen and Chairman Gottfried Haberler. (GATT, *Trends in International Trade, Report by a Panel of Experts*, 1958). The significance of this report lay in the fact that it shifted attention to the export side of the LDCs' trade problems. The Haberler Report, as it came to be known in honour of its Chairman, 'did not mince words' (Dam, 1970, p. 229). The substance of the report was that the predicament of LDCs was due in no small measure to the trade policies of the developed countries.

On the basis of these findings, the GATT inaugurated a Programme for the Expansion of International Trade under which the problems of economic development were brought under GATT's scrutiny. A committee was established, known as Committee III, to study the obstacles that restricted LDCs' exports into the developed market economies. The information gathered by Committee III was detailed and extensive but little was gained from it, except a Declaration on the Promotion of Trade of the Less Developed Countries at the 1961 Ministerial Meeting which made no concrete commitments and had negligible practical effect.

2.3.1 Reciprocity

Although the findings of the Haberler Report and Committee III did not have immediate practical impact, they provided the LDCs with detailed information to sustain their case for special treatment. The Haberler Report became the first landmark around which LDCs coalesced in the reform drive. A year after the publication of the Haberler Report, for the first time in GATT history, fifteen LDCs (Brazil, Burma, Cambodia, Chile, Cuba, Federation of Malaya, Federation of Rhodesia and Nyasaland, Ghana, Greece, India, Indonesia, Pakistan, Peru and Uruguay) met formally as a distinct group, and submitted a *Note on the Expansion of International Trade*. The Note pointed out that their capacity to participate in the central activity of the organization, i.e. tariff negotiation, was limited. Furthermore, their exports of primary products met other restrictions than tariffs. They therefore required negotiation on these NTMs. Moreover, as they could not do without tariffs for fiscal and development purposes (though a considerable proportion of their imports were capital goods not subject to appreciable tariffs), they proposed that the developed members should make unilateral concessions with a view to contributing to the rise in export earnings of the LDCs. (Curzon, 1965, p. 231).

The Note questioned the core principles of the GATT system—reciprocity and equality of treatment—collectively for the first time. It was the first collective plea put forth in GATT and it established the LDCs as a formal though very loose and open lobby. From then on countries would join the lobby or not, depending on the issue, but collective pressure became established practice. The more active countries kept up their individual exhortations. Among these was Chile. In 1961 the Chilean delegate Federico García Oldini proposed that LDCs be granted 'concessions without compensation' (GATT, SR 18/4, p. 52). Some time later, Chile also challenged the principal supplier procedure. García Oldini judged that 'the formula was unsuited to the needs of the LDCs because high tariffs in industrialized countries had often prevented the exports of the former from becoming principal suppliers . . . and that a new plan for tariff reductions should take less account of those criteria' (GATT, L/1768, 3 May 1962). The principal supplier rule and the reciprocity rule are in effect two sides of the same coin. To keep an eye on reciprocity, the principal supplier is the one made to 'pay' in kind for the concession. Chile was then voicing a generalized Latin American dissatisfaction with these mechanisms and the region's search for new formulae. Significantly, the Latin American Free Trade Area (LAFTA), established in 1960, had not incorporated either of these rules.

A less radical line was taken in 1963 by another set of twenty-one LDCs with some overlapping with the group that had previously submitted the Note in 1961. This new set included Argentina, Burma, Brazil, Cambodia, Ceylon, Cuba, Chile, Nigeria, Federation of Malaya, Ghana, Haiti, India, Indonesia, Israel, Pakistan, Peru, United Arab Republic, Tanganyika, Tunisia, Uruguay and Yugoslavia. Rather than rule reform, this group urged the extension of existing rules to excluded products. They proposed a *Programme of Action* urging the developed contracting parties to adopt the following measures on exports of LDCs:

(a) a commitment not to introduce new tariffs and non-tariff measures;
(b) the elimination of illegal quantitative restrictions on imports;
(c) duty-free entry for tropical products;
(d) a schedule for the reduction and elimination of tariffs on semi-processed and processed products;
(e) the elimination of internal taxes on products wholly or mainly produced in LDCs. (GATT, BISD, 12th S, p. 36).

The Programme called for the unilateral reduction of tariffs and NTMs that affected LDCs' exports, simply asking developed countries to commit themselves more fully to a 'GATT-type barrier-lowering approach' (Dam, 1970, p. 235).

Thus we see LDCs advancing on tariff rules on two fronts: on the one hand, reform of GAT rules, on the other, fuller implementation of GATT rules and principles as regards their own particular exports. These dispersed moves merely reflected the dissimilarity of their circumstances. At the same time as this call by some LDCs for freer trade on an MFN basis, the EEC was negotiating the Yaounde Convention with eighteen former African colonies (Burundi, Central African Republic, Cameroun, Chad, Congo (Brazzaville), Congo (Kinshasa), Dahomey, Gabon, Ivory Coast, Madagascar, Mali, Mauritania, Niger, Rwanda, Senegal, Somalia, Togo, Upper Volta). The purpose was to grant these newly independent states 'associate' status,[7] and thereby preferential tariff treatment. Of the twenty-one countries that called for the Programme of Action, none held associate status, and they feared that they would be bypassed by the institutionalization of a system of preferences that discriminated against them.

Accordingly, the Indian delegate, speaking for them all, objected that: 'The negotiations that are taking place with a view to association of the 18 African and Malagasy states with the EEC are a deviation from GATT rules.' (L/1902, November 1962, p. 1.)

The two proposals, the 1959 *Note on The Expansion of International Trade* and the 1963 Programme of Action had one point in common. Both urged unilateral reductions in favour of the LDCs. Pressures on this front reached a climax simultaneously with the preparations for the United Nations Conference on Trade and Development (UNCTAD). The LDCs, dissatisfied with the progress made in GATT to link their development problems to their commercial problems, had resorted to the United Nations forum to press for the calling of a conference to deal with world trade problems. The mere calling of such a conference meant a challenge to the GATT and its management of trade relations. Discussions on the implementation of the reforms and their legal status began in May 1963. In February 1965, eight months after the euphoric conclusion of UNCTAD I, the proposals were incorporated as a new chapter of the General Agreement, Part IV on *Trade and Development*.

Gosovic, who has made the most extensive enquiry into GATT–UNCTAD relations (1972) notes that Part IV was a nearly complete response to views on trade of the Final Act of UNCTAD I.[8] Prebisch's report to the UNCTAD had argued that the main flaw in the GATT was that it did not deal with the problem of international trade as part of the general problem of development. With Part IV there was explicit recognition that the disparate stages of economic development among the contracting parties was a factor to be taken into account.

The core innovation of Part IV is contained in Article XXXVI which specifies that 'developed countries do not expect reciprocity for commitments in trade negotiations to remove tariff and other barriers to the trade of the less developed contracting parties'. At the level of principle this introduced a radical change: it cast aside the notion that underpinned GATT of give-and-take betwen equally sovereign states and economies that were equally self-contained with ample scope for manœuvre in concession-swapping. The benefits that LDCs were to derive from their participation in GATT were in principle no longer assumed to depend on what they were able to offer in return.

Whether the reform was of more than symbolic importance was yet to be seen. The first practical test came during negotiations in the Kennedy Round (1964–7). At the conclusion of the Round, the Peruvian delegate spoke on behalf of the LDCs:

> Today when the Kennedy Round negotiations have come to an end, the developing countries participating in these negotiations wish to state that the most important problems of most of them in the field of trade taken up with the framework of these negotiations, still remain unresolved. These developing countries deeply regret that they are not in a position to share, to the same extent, the satisfaction of the developed countries at the conclusion and achievements of the Kennedy Round. [GATT, Press release No. 994, 30 June 1967.]

UNCTAD's evaluation was also pessimistic (1964, TD/6). Ernest Preeg, a member of the United States delegation, subsequently confirmed that 'because most of the accomplishments of the Kennedy Round were in areas where developing countries have smaller export interests, the benefits they derived were smaller' (Preeg, 1970, p. 227). The degree of cuts was significantly less than on trade among the industrialized countries, almost wholly because of the below-average results for textiles, iron and steel and processed agricultural goods—a pattern that was repeated in the Tokyo Round (GATT, 1979). The practical effect of non-reciprocity, the most significant innovation of Part IV, was far from satisfactory.

2.3.2 Preferences

LDCs nevertheless persisted in their diplomatic endeavours, now concentrating on the reforms to MFN, the other central feature of GATT's tariff rules. Two kinds of reforms to MFN have been discussed in the GATT: preferences by developed countries in favour of LDCs and preferential arrangements among LDCs themselves. In this section only the former will be dealt with. Preferences among LDCs, granted largely at a regional level, are discussed in detail in Chapter 5.

A consensus on the subject of preferences did not develop as smoothly or as promptly as it had done on the non-reciprocity issue. Preferences by developed countries for LDCs had been mentioned by the Haberler Report as a possibility to be studied. The negotiations leading to the incorporation of Part IV as well as to the creation of UNCTAD had also debated the topic. With a two-tier tariff system, one for LDCs, the other the MFN higher level, the LDCs' suppliers would overcome their handicaps in the competition with exports from developed countries. This it was believed would encourage export diversification and provide a basis for a second export-orientated stage of industrial growth.

Yet the relaxation of the MFN rule in the form of an amendment to Article I required unanimous agreement and not only did the issue separate LDCs and developed countries, but there were divisions within each camp as well. On the LDC side, the African countries that enjoyed preferential access to EEC markets were aware that they would probably lose this if the preferences were extended to all LDCs. More generally, there was a divergence of outlook among LDCs, depending upon their relative size and on the stage they had so far reached in the development of manufacturing industries. The least industrialized among them saw little likelihood that they would gain from generalized preferences under which they would have to compete on equal terms with, for example, India or Brazil (J. Evans, 1971, p. 122). Among the developed countries, the EEC, as we have seen, was sympathetic to the idea of granting preferences, though on a selective basis rather than to all LDCs indiscriminately. The United States was strongly opposed to the idea. Throughout the Kennedy Round, the American delegation had expressed the fear that to implement a system of preferences the MFN rate would be kept high so as to leave room for a 'margin of preference'.[9] In the United States there was also greater interest in remaining faithful to the founding vision of GATT which was thought to be working well. Discussion among the developed countries was conducted in the privacy of the OECD where the United States, after the conclusion of the Kennedy Round and before the UNCTAD II Conference in 1968, reversed its position.[10] However, a common approach to implementation was difficult to find and a set of guidelines only was agreed on at the OECD.

When the UNCTAD II met in New Delhi in 1968, developed and less developed countries were able to reach a tentative consensus for the establishment of a generalized system of preferences (GSP). After two years of negotiations, a firmer agreement was reached. The problem of the deviation from MFN obligation that this entailed was solved by a temporary compromise. On 25 June 1971, a 'waiver' for a ten-year period was granted in the GATT to provide developed countries with legal permission to depart from the MFN rule. The first scheme to be implemented shortly after was the European Community's, on 1 July 1971.

The initial proposal for a GSP had envisaged a common system giving all LDCs equal conditions of access in all developed countries. Because of the conflicts of interest on both sides this common approach could not be carried through. It was agreed that each preference-giving country should go its own way with the proviso that the OECD guidelines should be followed. What resulted, instead of a 'generalized system', was a cluster of country schemes with only a few common features. These common features can be summarized very briefly as follows. Each preference-giving country retains the right to select the recipient countries entitled to more favourable tariff treatment as well as the products to be covered. Preferential imports are subject to quantitative restrictions, i.e. ceiling limitations are imposed on either the volume or the value of a product entitled to access at a preferential rate. The EEC and the Japanese schemes have an aggregate ceiling for every product. The American scheme applies a country ceiling.

A further feature of the system as it evolved is that preferential tariffs are not bound as MFN tariffs are. Hence, a preferential concession can be withdrawn or the margin of preference reduced unilaterally, the affected country having no recourse to compensation or retaliation, as is the case with MFN tariffs bound within the GATT. In the cautious words of Olivier Long, former Director-General of the GATT, 'developing countries always took the view that this waiver approach was unwarranted and outmoded' (GATT, 1979, p. 98).

Dissatisfaction with the insecure status of the GSP led Brazil to put forward a plan to incorporate it into the GATT in a more integral way. The proposal was submitted in February 1977 in the course of the Tokyo Round. It was pointed out that because preferences are introduced *ex gratia*, they can also be withdrawn unilaterally without prior notification, and thus, cannot provide a sound basis for long-term investment. Two reforms were suggested 'in order to create an improved climate for investment' (Alvares Maciel, 1977, p. 8). The first aspect of the proposal was to bind preferential concessions in the same way as MFN concessions are bound. Once bound, preferences would be applied on a non-discriminatory basis to all LDCs. The second aspect was that LDCs, instead of waiting to be granted preferences, would negotiate for them; the parties most interested in getting a preference would offer in return a concession to the preference-granting country which would then be extended on a MFN basis to all other developed members of GATT. This, Brazil believed, would provide a sound legal basis for negotiations and would contribute to transforming LDCs from passive recipients of tariff concessions into active, fully-fledged members.

The outcome of the negotiations on these issues was disappointing to the LDCs. The major result of the Tokyo Round in this respect was the modest one that a waiver would no longer be required by developed countries granting preferences to LDCs or by LDCs negotiating preferences among themselves. This agreement was put together in the form of an 'Enabling Clause' which allows developed countries to provide 'differential and more

le treatment' to LDCs without extending such treatment to other
ng parties. Such differential treatment covers the GSP as well as the
following aspects of LDC trade: (a) the use of non-tariff measures to protect
the home market; (b) the granting of mutual preferences within regional or
global trade arrangements among LDCs; and (c) special treatment for the
least developed LDCs (GATT, 1979).

Security of access under preferential cover was not attained; neither were
innovations introduced to make preferential concessions negotiable. Not only
have the LDCs failed to achieve provisions for binding preferential concessions or preferential margins, but also, consequently, they have not
obtained the right to claim compensation if modifications occur.

Furthermore, at the conclusion of the Tokyo Round, UNCTAD noted that
the cuts negotiated in MFN duties had reduced the average margin of
preference by 50 per cent (UNCTAD, 1979, TD/227, pp. 12–13). Moreover,
in practice the actual gains for LDCs have been limited by the narrow product
coverage, by ceilings on either volume or value and restrictive rules of origin.
Only a small proportion of LDCs' exports into the developed countries are
carried out under preferential cover. It has been estimated that in 1980 nearly
50 per cent of the total dutiable OECD imports from LDCs was eligible for
GSP treatment; yet only 21 per cent of those imports in fact received such
treatment (UNCTAD, 1983, TD/274, p. 7).

2.4 WIDER TRENDS

Since the immediate post-war years LDCs' attitudes *vis-à-vis* the GATT
seemed to have proceeded on a double track. On the one hand, their
discontent with the functioning of GATT grew, and as it became more
articulate it led to the organization of UNCTAD. On the other hand, governments showed that they did not dismiss the value of GATT altogether. Membership has grown continuously, and participation in discussions and
negotiations has also increased. Several factors may account for this enhanced
activity.

In the 1950s and 1960s, on the whole, LDCs were largely exporters of
primary products. Since the GATT had excluded agricultural products, raw
materials and fisheries from tariff reduction negotiations and had also
removed price stabilization schemes from its sphere of influence, the prevailing perception among LDCs was that little had resulted from GATT
membership—except for pressures on them to maintain an acceptable degree
of free access to their domestic markets. It is noteworthy that at the time of
GATT's inception in 1947, few of the already independent LDCs joined.

At that time, in some of the relatively more advanced LDCs, policies of
industrialization by import substitution were being pushed. In its initial

stages this industrialization process was orientated mainly towards supplying the domestic market, and required a certain degree of insulation from foreign competition. As the process of industrialization took off and LDCs became more competitive in certain sectors, they began to seek improved access to foreign markets and, as a result, stepped up participation in the GATT.

Furthermore, UNCTAD failed to become a world-wide trade institution to supersede the GATT, but thanks in part to its efforts and its proposals for 'trade rather than aid' as the road towards development, some changes in the rules were achieved. However, disjointed any efforts at GATT reform may have been, the mere existence of the UNCTAD meant a constant flow of demands, proposals and information at the disposal of LDCs—which improved and encouraged their participation in trade negotiations. Since the adoption of Part IV, 'commercial policy to aid development became part of the GATT doctrine' (Curzon, 1965, p. 258).

Despite these changes in favour of the LDCs, dissatisfaction with the functioning of the GATT persisted. Often LDCs complaints seemed to arise from a belief that there was a conspiracy against them. During the Tokyo Round, for instance,

> delegations from a number of developing countries expressed concern about the lack of opportunities for their involvement in the negotiating process under the multilateral trade negotiations . . . Decisions were being taken by a small group of countries . . . often outside the multilateral trade negotiations and not in Geneva. [GATT, Com. TD/100, August 1978, p. 11.]

Alongside this kind of complaint, LDCs continued to make pleas for better commercial treatment. Market access was requested on the grounds of the benefits that the international community as a whole was to derive from redressing trade inequities and from grappling with the problems of under-development. LDCs aimed to demonstrate both the gravity of their problems and the possibility of meeting their claims without necessarily bringing about major disruptions in the developed economies.

While LDCs concentrated their efforts to obtain positive discrimination, they were unwary of the opposite trend to discriminate against them that began to gather force. Initially the measures went unnoticed, perhaps because they seemed to be mainly directed at Japan at the time of its accession to GATT, or perhaps because they were seen as merely temporary deviations. From 1961 the GATT institutionalized a special regime to regulate textile exports from low- to higher-wage countries. First there came the Short Term Arrangement Regarding International Trade in Cotton Textiles (STA), and then the Long Term Arrangement (LTA), covering the 1962–7 period. The regime withdrew this flow of trade from the GATT system of tariff control and placed it under a parallel system of quota control specified by country of origin, country of destination and product category. The quotas were to be set on a bilateral basis, thus overtly violating the principle of non-discrimination. From this time forward, the flow of trade, from low-wage LDCs to high-wage developed countries, became subject to increasingly discriminating measures. The LTA was renewed in 1967 for a further three-year period and in 1970 for a further four years. In 1974 it was extended to cover wool and man-made fibres in addition to cotton textiles and so became known thenceforth as the Multi-Fibre Agreement (MFA).

During the Kennedy Round, the LDCs, by then dissatisfied with the restrictive and discriminatory features of the LTA, pressed for revisions to liberalize it. The United States, the EEC and other developed countries insisted on an extension of the LTA, then due to expire in September 1967, as a condition of any tariff reductions in textiles. In the final days of the Round (June 1967) the EEC, followed by the United States, threatened that tariffs might 'snap back' to their former levels if the LTA were to be discontinued. The modest cuts offered in this sector (in the order of 20 per cent as opposed to the average reduction of 35 to 39 per cent) were conditional to the further extension of the LTA (Preeg, 1970, pp. 106, 198). LDCs rejected this offer because they could anticipate that any potential increase in their exports through tariff cuts would be frustrated by quotas; so the prospect of tariff cuts could not be seen as adequate inducement. In the end the developed countries offered improved quotas to individual exporting countries as a more persuasive form of payment (J. Evans, 1971, p. 232).[11] The Kennedy Round thus concluded with MFN tariff cuts on textiles—albeit below average—and an extension of quotas for LDCs.

A similar set of circumstances arose during the Tokyo Round. This time President Carter promised his textile lobby that offers of tariff reductions on an MFN basis would also be extended on a 'snap back' condition. Should the LDCs fail to renew the MFA, tariffs would snap back to the pre-Tokyo Round levels. The 'snap back' condition has aggravated the discriminatory nature of these regulations, given that while the process of tariff reductions continues on an MFN basis, the quota system is *only* applied against LDCs—described as sources of 'market disruption'.

Although discriminatory practices against LDCs are most prominent in the textile sector, other sectors have not been exempt. The Commonwealth Secretariat has noted that

> In the case of manufactures what has been achieved so painfully in lower tariffs has for many developing countries been altogether offset, and more than offset, by quantitative limitations that are most severe where the developing countries have proved most successful . . . The new barriers to trade that have grown up in the industrialized countries apply with special

force to the manufactured exports of those countries and are highly discriminatory. [Commonwealth Secretariat 1982, pp. 7, 17.]

Despite these setbacks, LDCs continued to have some success at the level of principles and declarations. The Declaration signed at the conclusion of the 1982 Ministerial Meeting states that:

> In drawing up the work programme and priorities for the 1980s, the Contracting Parties undertake, individually and jointly . . .to ensure the effective implementation of GATT rules and provisions and specifically those concerning the developing countries, thereby furthering the dynamic role of developing countries in international trade. [GATT, *Focus*, December 1982, p. 3.]

Explanations of the discrimination against the LDCs are broadly of two types. One hinges on diplomatic circumstances. From a narrowly commercial perspective, the exclusion of LDCs from the benefits of GATT, the limited scope of the reforms, as well as their marginal impact, have usually been attributed to LDCs' 'lack of expertise and negotiating skills' (personal interview with former Director-General Olivier Long, 13 November 1980) or to their failure to attract the developed countries with real bargaining counters. As Bergsten and Cline put it:

> An inherent limitation on the bargaining strength of developing countries in past rounds of trade negotiations has been the lack of liberalisation offers of their own to serve as bargaining chips. Indeed the . . . concept that developing countries provide 'automatic reciprocity' because they spend virtually all the foreign exchange they earn on imports, largely from the industrial countries, while broadly true, has meant a lack of bargaining power. [Bergsten & Cline, 1982, p. 29.]

This line of argument has several problematic features however. No doubt the LDCs have limited bargaining power. This is almost a truism. The real question that must be addressed relates to how bargaining power is attained, since bargaining power is the product of underlying economic factors rather than the cause of these factors. Moreover, taking the element of bargaining power as the central explanatory factor rather than as a contingent one, is almost like taking an apologetic view of the issue. Implicitly, what is being said is that if negotiators were more skilful, LDCs would get a better deal. This is the counterpart to the LDCs' conspiracy theory, casting the blame back on their inadequacies. Furthermore, the prescription that follows from the diagnosis is lacking in realism. The argument is that LDCs do not have bargaining power because unfortunately, although they give all they have, others do not value it. The solution is seen as a question of forgetting the valueless reciprocity they offer and offering more access to their own markets. Now if LDCs spend virtually all their foreign exchange on imports, how would they obtain the additional funds for those additional imports they ought to be absorbing as bargaining chips? Lastly, an explanation too narrowly centred on bargaining power can neither explain why trade has not been liberalized *among* LDCs although they could be seen as having roughly equivalent bargaining power, nor why different export sectors of LDCs receive different treatment in the markets of developed countries.

The other explanation of discrimination against LDCs is more strictly economic in the sense that it refers to forces which operate regardless of bargaining skills or expertise. The latter, on this line of thought, are contingent factors that can enhance or undermine a given constellation of objective possibilities but cannot by themselves significantly alter secular trends in the world economy. The following chapter will develop this line and attempt to see behind the phenomenon of bargaining power to take into account what factors operate and produce it. It will look at the character of world trade and the pattern of liberalization since World War II. It will seek there the fundamental causes of the failure to integrate LDCs into the GATT and of the discrimination against them. Subsequent chapters will then illustrate how these trends affect, on the one hand, the textile sector of all LDCs, and on the other, the integration attempts of the Latin American Free Trade Area.

NOTES

1. For a brief review of the classical and neo-classical models, see Stein (1984), especially Chapters 1 and 2.
2. The first landmarks are: United Nations, *The Economic Development of Latin America and its Principal Problems* (by Raúl Prebisch) E/CN.12/89/Rev. 1, New York, 1950 (Spanish edition, 1949) and United Nations, *Economic Survey of Latin America*, 1949 E/CN.12/164/Rev.1, New York, 1951.
3. Hans W. Singer, 'The distribution of gains between investing and borrowing countries', *American Economic Review, Papers and Proceedings*, Vol. II, No. 2, 1950.
4. The most comprehensive study on the subject is contained in the Proceedings of UNCTAD I. Most of the issues have been summarized in Gosovic (1972).
5. The waiver would have an additional detrimental effect on LDCs' textile exports, as we shall see in Chapter 4.
6. The Havana Charter contained a whole chapter on 'Intergovernmental Commodity Agreements'.
7. Part IV of the Treaty of Rome gives former colonies the right to 'association' with the EEC. This involves reciprocal preferences between the EEC and the associated state, access to a multilateral aid fund and joint institutions (Treaty of Rome, Part IV, Articles 131–6).
8. The exception was the plea for a generalized system of preferences which was discussed at UNCTAD but remained unsatisfied until 1971.

9. The margin of preference is the difference between the MFN tariff and the rate applied to imports from LDC beneficiaries.
10. For an analysis of the American policy reversal see Ronald I. Meltzer, *The Politics of Policy Reversal: the American Response to the Issue of Granting Preferences to the Developing Countries, 1964–1967*, unpublished PhD dissertation (Colombia University, 1975).
11. John Evans was a member of the American delegation to the Kennedy Round. His book, like Preeg's, offers detailed insiders' views of those negotiations.

3   The character of world trade

3.1 INTRODUCTION

This chapter comprises an analysis of the main developments in the structure of international trade since the war; it attempts to provide some pointers to underlying trends that have affected the LDCs' position in the GATT. Before commencing this task, it may be of some value to supplement the interpretation by referring the reader briefly to history. Historically considered, trade liberalization has not been a product of negotiation. To take a major example, in particular, late nineteenth-century and early twentieth-century British manufacturing interests were seen to be best served by a policy of unilateral free trade or low tariffs on wage goods and industrial inputs. Then the major concern was to ensure the cheapest possible supplies for price-competitive industries. Export markets were opened less by negotiation than by conquest or by unequal treaties imposing free trade on overseas territories, as a result of which many native craft industries disappeared (Bagchi, 1982; A. G. Frank, 1967).

With the foundation of GATT, a bargaining style of trade liberalization was instituted. The economic literature at the time GATT was created anticipated industrial development to proceed by price competition and geographical relocation. The neo-classical approach to international trade held that international specialization or division of labour is the reason why international trade takes place and brings mutual benefit. Exchanges of wine for cloth and tea for pharmaceuticals were explained by disparities in natural resources and relative costs of production. Since differences in factor endowments give rise to trade, the theory anticipated that under free-trade conditions trade would be greater between dissimilar economies. The expectation was therefore that division of labour according to cost differentials would lead to industry X expanding in one country and contracting elsewhere, while the opposite would happen to industry Y; hence the provision in GATT for the process to be one of gradual and reciprocal accommodation if trade wars and colonialism, as in the past, were to be averted.

Given the expectation that the freeing of trade would lead to a process whereby industries would be changing geographical location as patterns of comparative advantages shifted globally, and yet at the same time a great concern with maintaining full employment, GATT codified a system which was not one of absolute free trade but offered a second best. Domestic interests would be allowed a degree of protection or preferential treatment over foreigners, but the latter could compete for a *part* of the domestic market. How large a share of the market the foreign supplier could reasonaby claim was, however, never explicitly defined. In relations between LDCs and developed countries the issue became a bone of contention.

The fear of vulnerability to changes in comparative advantage is reflected in GATT's safeguard clause, Article XIX. The purpose of Article XIX was to allow a country to withdraw a tariff concession, should it find that the increased flow of imports it allowed was intolerably large and hurting its domestic producers.

3.2 INTRA-INDUSTRY TRADE AND INDUSTRIAL CONVERGENCE

In contrast to expectations, the accelerated growth of world trade since the war has not reflected the simple exchange of wine for cloth, i.e. the standardized goods of competitive firms for which wide differences in national production costs can be held. By the 1960s it became apparent that the growth of trade among industrial countries did not lead to polarization, with industries expanding here at the cost of contraction there.

> Instead, the X industry would expand in all the countries which participated in the freeing of trade, and the Y industry too would have a similar experience in those countries. Although the freeing of trade did lead to growth of trade of the cloth for wine (of X for Y) variety, as expected, it led to even more growth of trade for the X for X (or cloth for cloth) variety. [Meyer, 1978, p. 23.]

The notion of comparative advantage in its traditional form could no longer account for what was happening in trade relations between industrial countries.

More than 80 per cent of world trade, as well as two-thirds of world output, is generated by the industrial countries (GATT, 1982, p. 7) and these countries, rather than reflecting the tendency towards specialization and divergent economic structures, are marked by growing similarities in the broad pattern of their national economies. This structural convergence can be seen not only in the distribution of output and employment between agriculture, industry and services: it applies as well to the distribution of subsectors within industry. Therefore the mutual trade of these countries, the greater part of world trade, cannot be comfortably accounted for by disparities in natural resources, human endowments or economic development. Saunders' (1975) study of Western Europe, where industrial tariffs have reached negligible levels, points out that differences exist between advanced countries in technological capacity, in skills, in design, and in forms of industrial organization and marketing methods, but these are narrow and rapidly diminishing.

> It is not easy to explain the patterns of trade by differences in the relative costs, or availability of capital and labour—the structural factors generally taken as determining the comparative advantages in trade of different economies, and directing their respective specialisations. [p. 24]

The structural convergence of these countries means that their trade consists of exchanges within the same general categories of manufactured products, such as textiles for textiles or chemicals for chemicals. This is commonly known as intra-industry trade, whereby each country is both an exporter and an importer of the same broad range of products. To illustrate the dimensions of this two-way trade in Western Europe, Saunders points out the proportion of trade within given product groups that is bilaterally balanced (exports matched by imports). The table below also indicates that rather than adjusting trade of X for Y, or cloth for chemicals, trade liberalization during the ten-year period covered increased the proportion of bilateral balanced exchanges. Tariff cuts realized the potential for a higher level of reciprocal intra-industry trade rather than triggering geographical relocation. Grubel and Lloyd calculated that 71 per cent of the total growth in trade among EEC countries between 1959 and 1967 took the form of an increase in intra-industry trade.

Prior to liberalization, 53 per cent of total EEC trade was already intra-industry (Grubel & Lloyd, 1975, p. 135). Liberalization was not coupled with greater national specialization in the production and export of individual industries as had been expected but with the growth of trade in products belonging to the same industry. The similarity of material input requirements of the products from the same industry and the quite similar resource

Table 3.1 Bilaterally balanced proportion of trade turnover between 16 West European countries

	1959	1968
	%	%
Chemicals	50	65
Textiles	41	64
Non-electrical machinery	40	50

Source: Saunders, 1975, p. 25.

endowments dilutes the significance or the traditional notion of comparative advantage. It cannot be applied to exchange of goods within industries in the same way as with exchange between industries.

This process, though more manifest among EEC countries where tariffs have reached their lowest level, has also occurred in the trade of the OECD area as a whole. Grubel and Lloyd estimated that as long ago as the Kennedy Round more than half of the total export trade of the major industrial countries was accounted for by intra-industry trade. Japan and Australia showed well below average figures. On the other hand, Great Britain had above average intra-industry trade even before acceding to the EEC (Table 3.2)

Table 3.2 Intra-industry trade as share of total exports, 1967

	%		%
Canada	48	West Germany	46
United States	49	France	65
Japan	21	Italy	42
Belgium-Luxemburg	63	Great Britain	69
Netherlands	56	Australia	17

Mean: 55 %.
Source: Grubel & Lloyd, 1975, Table 3.1, p. 35.

With intra-industry trade, world trade in manufactures has grown at a much faster rate than production, as is evidenced in Table 3.3.[12]

The implication to be drawn from the facts set out is that trade among industrial countries:

> is determined only to a small extent by comparative advantages of the traditional kind. The *relative* labour costs, capital costs, etc. of manufacturing one description of machine tool rather than another are rarely likely to be very different between Britain and West Germany. The pattern of two-way trade seems likely to be determined rather by such factors as the special technical advantages of individual producing firms, their marketing capacity, or the state of their order books, and by the particular preferences and requirements of individual customers. [Saunders, 1975, p. 28.]

This is related to factor mobility and to a process known as product differentiation, to be discussed in the following sections. Trade has been harmoniously coupled with an increasingly fine degree of industrial specialization rather than with the threat of dislocation and 'runaway factories'.

Table 3.3 Evolution of world exports and production
(1963 = 100)

	1963	1973	1983
World exports of manufactures	100	280	429
World manufactured output	100	197	259

Source: GATT, *International Trade*, 1984, Appendix.

Trade liberalization among developed countries has thus not required or forced the shrinking of whole industrial sectors because of wide differences in comparative costs. Shonfield's review of international economic relations of the Western world confirms that the tariff-cutting of the 1950s and 1960s were relatively painless exercises. If judged in terms of their impact on employment in the countries concerned, Shonfield could not identify a case in which a net increase or decrease in the overall level of employment in any industrial country during this period could plausibly be held to have been caused by a particular change in import duties. 'No government lowers tariff barriers in the belief that it might raise the number of unemployed.' (Shonfield, 1976, p. 39).

Owing to this structural convergence of industrial countries with its high level of reciprocal intra-industry trade as far as their mutual trade is concerned, the resource reallocation effect of the lowering of industrial tariffs was relatively small. Orthodox discussions of trade policies of developed countries have tended to magnify 'the autonomous or trigger role of tariffs from which certain resource allocation decisions are supposed to follow.' (Díaz Alejandro, 1975, p. 94). W. M. Corden has similarly postulated that the importance of changes in various international trade policies, such as Britain joining or not joining the Common Market, or of a country reducing tariffs unilaterally by, say, 50 per cent, has been 'much over-rated'. (Corden, 1965, p. 51). Under these conditions the reduction of most industrial tariffs is of 'relative unimportance' (ibid.). This provided the GATT with a ready basis of operations. Other factors have also diminished the trigger role of tariffs and have facilitated the task of the GATT. To these we now turn.

3.3 TECHNOLOGY AND THE CHANGING STRUCTURE OF THE MARKET

Central to the potential for a high level of reciprocal intra-industry trade is the pace of technological innovation in the twentieth century. Large sectors of manufacturing industry have become research and development-intensive. Research and development require capital investment and take time, which is also costly. This, in addition to the specialized technological expertise involved, implies that participation in the market has become restricted to fewer sellers. Potential entrants are no longer numerous or anonymous. With the rise of this bar to entry the price-competitive 'free market' declined relative to competition or quality terms or to the differentiation of the product sold. A differentiated product is defined as:

> a collection of functionally similar goods produced by competing sellers, but with each seller's product distinguishable from its rival by minor physical variations, brand name and subjective distinctions created by advertising, or differences in the ancillary terms and conditions of sale. [Caves in Shonfield, 1976, p. 129.]

Technology has led to increased product differentiation as well as to continual product innovation; this tends to concentrate production in larger firms which can cover the necessary capital outlays. Differentiated products by definition compete in style, quality or model, rather than simply price, and this feature potentially allows sectorially balanced trade between countries, the exchange of Fords for Austins and Renaults for VWs. Thus, product differentiation together with product innovation also contributed to altering the nature of modern trade without affecting the geographical location of industrial plants.

Increasing research intensity implies increasing capital costs in both relative and absolute terms. The quest to reduce production costs led to market expansion. Firms that had acquired and developed the technological expertise were bound to apply it in several product lines, and so become multiple-product firms. But this competitive edge could also be applied profitably by reproducing their domestic business in foreign markets, a feature that will be dealt with in the next section. Firms became not only multi-product, but multi-national as well; a process whereby increasing segments of the domestic and international market were transformed. Both large-scale corporations and intra-industry trade tend to be closely connected and to converge in technology-intensive sectors. Giant corporations are of course not only to be found in such sectors but these sectors do require heavy capital investment that can only be covered by large firms with high rates of self-finance.

Technology-intensive sectors do not all have equal potential for intra-industry trade. Meyer (1978) identifies three conditions that allow intra-industry trade. Intra-industry trade will mostly emerge in research and development-intensive sectors, but particularly in those goods with a short market life relative to the length of the gestation stage. For instance, the scope is greater in the electronic sector where products such as calculators and recorders take a long time in development but then (the models at least) have a short market life, than in traditional chemicals such as sulphuric acid which remain marketable for longer. The second condition facilitating intra-industry trade is increased specialization between plants within each product range. To take the example of the home computer Apple whose itinerary was traced by an article in the *Guardian*:[2] the metal is produced in a factory in West Germany; different microchips are produced by plants in California and Japan; then a workshop in Singapore separates those chips from the wafers of silicon on which they are built and mounts them individually; the power supplies for the computer are made by a factory in Taiwan, the keyboards by a plant in Cork. The multiple components are assembled in another factory in Cork (*The Guardian*, 12 May 1983, p. 16).[3] The third condition is that the use and user of the product can be identified at a point of production. To take the same example of the computer, the plant manufacturing the keyboards or any other component does so under precise specification from the user rather than for an anonymous market. Even if producer and user are separate firms, they have close links to establish production runs, design, etc. What is implied here is that production takes place under increasing returns to scale, that trade grows by more than production and finally that the goods produced are differentiated rather than standardized.

This structure of production and trade has been accompanied by a central change in the nature of the market: the degree of concentration of industrial production increased while the anonymity of both users and suppliers decreased. It can no longer be said that the hand of the market is invisible. Grubel and Lloyd's study of intra-industry trade points out that 'economies of scale in production are responsible for this trade' (Grubel & Lloyd, 1975, p. 150). Meyer stresses the role of research and development as the key factor. Both these factors are in practice difficult to disentangle: economies of scale and technology are features of the multi-product, multi-locational corporations. Economies of scale develop in oligopolistic markets where competition occurs less through changes in production prices than through product innovation, improvement, advertising and other methods not reflected in unit price indices. In the consumer goods market buyers are influenced by style and brand and are susceptible to persuasive advertising. Thus the goods produced by different countries hold market shares in terms of these qualities, not merely their price. The same holds for components and parts though a greater role is played by the end-user by means of laying down specifications for production. National specialization is then partial, so that no country specializes wholly in one or two products, nor does production of any single good concentrate in one country. Partial specialization and exchange of goods *within* rather than *between* industries is both cause and consequence of the 'structural convergence' of developed countries. Their economies have become closely intertwined and this has led to a situation in which countries are dependent on one another not only as export outlets but as purveyors of special products and components.

The Character of World Trade 45

In contrast, the trade of LDCs is concentrated much more heavily in raw materials, semi-manufactures and other staples, providing relatively less scope for product differentiation. Moreover, in these countries manufacturing sectors are small and competition through product differentiation is not as prevalent as in developed countries.

It follows that there are broadly two types of goods that show little responsiveness to intra-industry trade: primary commodities and the standardized products of traditional industries such as steel and clothing or industries that are natural resource based, such as cotton goods, and processed foods, drinks, tobacco, forestry products, etc. They are not primarily technology-intensive sectors and, especially in primary production, the goods produced by numerous suppliers can be virtually perfect substitutes for each other. The same is true to a lesser extent of textiles and steel. Product differentiation is less feasible and comparative costs play a greater role in the trade in such goods. The trade in these goods is of the traditional cloth for wine variety. If production costs between countries differ widely, free trade leads to expansion in one country at the expense of contraction elsewhere. With wide cost differentials, trade threatens to displace the higher-cost producer. While in intra-industry trade, trade causes increased output and grows faster than production, in inter-industrial trade there is no such link and in fact production may exceed trade, leading then not to more trade but to the blocking of trade, surplus capacity and trade conflicts.[4] We shall see in the following chapters how these factors operated in the textile exports of LDCs to developed countries and in the integration efforts of the Latin American countries.

World trade in manufactures concentrates in sectors that are relatively highly capital-intensive, rather than resource or labour-intensive (Table 3.4). It is natural that GATT has tended to be most effective and that negotiations

Table 3.4 Commodity composition of world trade in manufactures (%)

	1937	1950	1959	1973	1980
Engineering	26.5	34.9	41.3	49.6	54.0
machinery & equipment	(16)	(20.7)	(24.8)	(36.8)	(41.5)
transport	(10)	(14.2)	(16.5)	(12.7)	(12.5)
Textiles & clothing	21.5	19.9	11.1	8.1	8.7
Metals (iron & steel)	15.3	12.9	13.5	11.5	7.0
Chemicals	10.6	10.5	12.0	12.3	14.0
All others	26.0	21.9	22.1	18.5	16.3
	100%	100%	100%	100%	100%

Source: Kenwood & Lougheed, *The Growth of the International Economy* and *GATT, International Trade*, 1983.

have gone further and more smoothly where there has been a potential for intra-industry trade. It is true that there have been reductions in tariffs in agriculture, textiles and steel, but these have little significance where governments intervene actively to regulate production and to set prices, or have negotiated strictly monitored quotas to offset the effect of lower tariffs.

In his review of the Kennedy Round (1964–7), Preeg observed that, 'The largest reductions were achieved in industries typified by advanced technology, product innovation and large, often international, firms.' Preeg, however, was puzzled, because, 'Somewhat paradoxically, many industries show the potential for the clearest gains from trade in the classical comparative advantage sense', such a textiles, leather, rubber and steel, are the sectors in which reductions in trade barriers were less easily accommodated, and correspondingly smaller reductions were accomplished (Preeg, 1970, p. 257). This trend was repeated in the Tokyo Round which achieved less than average reductions in such sectors (GATT, 1979, p. 120). These are price-sensitive, decreasing returns activities. In these activities a reluctance to liberalize prevails, and this is so precisely because of the scope that exists for the emigration of industries. Preeg's first-hand experience as a United States negotiator during the Kennedy round led him to conclude that the potential for tariff elimination varies from sector to sector and that the most likely candidates for freer trade are those sectors where large and dynamic firms are involved and for which complete elimination of tariffs 'could provide important economic gains with relatively little adverse impact on individual producers or nations' (Preeg, 1970, p. 265). Preeg's conclusion was based on his insight into actual negotiations; it could not explain the 'paradox' that liberalization was obstructed when the gains from trade were greatest. Meyer's analysis, relying on the evidence of intra-industry trade, leads to the same conclusion, now deprived of perplexity. The reciprocal freeing of trade has proved more far-reaching where the conditions of intra-industry trade are satisfied. If competition from foreign producers threatens domestic sectors, liberalization will be resisted and GATT's role will be obstructed.

3.4   INTERNATIONALIZATION OF PRODUCTION

Intimately related to the changes described above, another structural factor contributed to the dynamism of trade liberalization: the sustained and unprecedented expansion of transnational investment, a process commonly described as the internationalization of capital. By the time the Bretton Woods rules broke down, with the declaration of dollar inconvertibility in 1971, the greater part of world output that was placed in the world market was no longer produced, as noted above, by fragmented small-scale firms. World output was largely internationalized through the agency of multinational corporations (MNCs). It has been calculated that as far back as 1971 the output of enterprises owned and controlled by parent companies outside the country in which the production occurred amounted to some $330 billion. This internationalized production compares with a total value of world exports in the same year of £310 billion. The figures are only meant to show the relative magnitude of each notion. It should be stressed that not all international production enters international trade. International production takes into account the output of the foreign affiliates of MNCs, whether it enters international trade or not. The foreign affiliates of multinational corporations (i.e. internationalized capital) accounted for about one-third of all international trade (Shonfield, 1976, p. 115).

The lead in internationalizing production was taken by American business and this spread rapidly abroad after the end of the war until the devaluation of the dollar in the early 1970s, at which point one half of international production was related to American-based firms. 'The US was, in fact, the only country which exported less from its domestic territory than was exported by its enterprises located abroad.' (Shonfield, 1976, p. 115). Not only did this internationalization affect the world economy: in terms of the American economy itself, an extensive United Nations study estimated that the value of American international production was four times the magnitude of American exports. In Switzerland it was nearly two-and-a-half times the magnitude and for Britain it was 2.15, but for West Germany and Japan, a negligible 0.37. It appears that the relative competitiveness of goods produced in West Germany and Japan made it more attractive for firms to export from home base than to engage in overseas production; while for the United States and, to a lesser extent, Great Britain and Switzerland, the opposite situation held (Table 3.5).

Table 3.5 International production
as a share of exports

United States	3.96
Switzerland	2.36
Great Britain	2.15
France	0.95
Sweden	0.92
Canada	0.68
Netherlands	0.52
Italy	0.44
Japan	0.37
West Germany	0.37

Source: UN, *Multinational Corporations in World Development*, New York, 1973.

As was noted in the previous section, the most dynamic sectors of production are technology-based and these were the sectors that first achieved preeminence in the United States and at a later stage in Europe and Japan. 'When exports became substantial firms tended to establish subsidiaries abroad.' (Meyer, 1978, p. 32). Successful exporters became multinational, and multinationals were active exporters. Their competitive edge was exploited by exporting goods as well as the factor of production that enjoyed greatest mobility, i.e. capital.

Firms with overseas affiliates accounted for about 70 per cent of total American exports (US Senate, 1973, pp. 278–9). For Britain, Meyer noted a similar share: firms with foreign branches contributed to over 75 per cent of British exports in the early 1970s.

Post-1971 currency realignments induced other successful exporting countries to accelerate the pace of outward investment and production. In fact the lack of West German and Japanese foreign investment for a long time after World War II can largely be explained in terms of the rapid internal growth of the two economies and the fact that the undervaluation of their currencies 'favoured the exploitation of foreign markets by exports rather than by outward direct investment.' (Dunning, 1973, p. 330). Relative rates of growth, rates of exchange and rates of profit are all incentives for capital to extend abroad.

Dunning also notes that the interest of firms in internationalizing and the degree to which it is undertaken is related to the type of goods produced by the firms. Goods that are easily tradeable or easily assimilated abroad, such as woollens, footwear, cutlery, etc., show a low ratio of foreign production to exports from their home base. In other words, there tends to be only marginal foreign direct investment in such goods, production of which remains mainly in the hands of native companies.

Where more arcane technology is involved, as in motor cars and electronic goods, there is a high ratio of foreign production to exports. In some segments of the consumer electronics business (portable radios, televisions, car radios, cassette and tape recorders), British as well as American firms have virtually transferred all of the production of such goods abroad and have become net importers of their own foreign production into their home territory (Cable, 1983).

A second factor closely related to the type of goods is the organization of markets. If production is unconcentrated, foreign production may be uneconomical; more concentrated markets would invite it. In competetive markets such as cotton textiles, woollens, cutlery and leather goods, for which the technical know-how required is relatively simple and easily diffused, production tends to be dispersed; these do not attract foreign capital to the same extent as chemicals or motor cars.

It follows that there is a close correspondence between the sectors where foreign investment flows and those sectors more responsive to intra-industry trade. Both are related to oligopolistic production, product differentiation and economies of scale. These trends resulted in the industrial convergence noted by Saunders. The mobility of capital, intra-industry trade and industrial convergence combined to integrate the Western world into 'a magic circle of self-sustaining exchanges' (Shonfield, 1976,p. 108).

Trade and capital flows have become inextricably connected to such an extent that some analysts believe that 'the classroom distinction between the current and capital accounts (and the corresponding separation between policies towards trade and capital flows) is becoming increasingly irrelevant in world markets dominated by multi-national corporations'. (Díaz Alejandro, 1975, p. 94). Lamfalussy also suggests that 'In practice, both the statistician and the government agency in charge of foreign exchange controls will find it exceedingly difficult to distinguish trade from capital flows.' (Shonfield, 1976, p. 117).

As with international trade, the dominant direction that the flow of capital has taken is from one industrial country to another, with the declining share going to LDCs. Of global foreign direct investment, three-quarters are concentrated in developing countries (compared with two-thirds in the mid-1960s).[5] Flows to LDCs are comparatively small for most industrialized countries—with the striking exception of Japan, the bulk of whose investments are concentrated in South-east Asia. During the period 1966–77 foreign direct investment from the United States to the less developed countries amounted to 14 per cent of its total flows, for the United Kingdom 19 per cent, for West Germany and France 30 per cent each, while it reached 60 per cent for Japan (World Bank, 1979, pp. 4 and 5). Thus, in broad terms, while trade and investment flows rendered industrialized countries increasingly integrated or 'interdependent' (with Japan less so), an evident fracture between these and LDCs persisted.

Though capital mobility was the underlying bedrock for the growth of trade, influencing composition and direction of flows, not all international production enters international trade, nor is all international production a driving force for more or freer trade. Where MNCs have expanded to defend market shares abroad, regardless of costs of operation, the link between growth of investment and trade is less direct.

In the race to attract foreign investment, LDCs have competed with each other to offer favourable terms for a declining share of global foreign investment. Foreign investment was seen as providing the country with the capacity to develop the capital and technology-intensive sectors. Among such incentives were high tariffs to protect the sectors considered dynamic in the 1960s, notably chemicals and motor vehicles. It was believed to be better to sacrifice efficiency and to have several MNCs competing with each other, even if markets were too small to realize economies of scale rather than allow monopoly benefits to just one foreign company. As pointed out by Sidney Dell, many firms deliberately built up capacity in each individual market in the certainty that competitors would be doing the same to defend market shares with the result that rates of utilization tended to be extremely low and hence unit costs very high across the industry. Even without over-capacity, such plants tended to be small by world standards and could not take advantage of economies of scale. Diseconomies of scale in turn made it necessary to maintain a high level of protection. Such industrial investment in LDCs 'was then dragged into the well-known vicious circle of low output, high costs and inflated protection' (Dell, 1966, p. 189).[6] Corroborating evidence of the high-cost, high-tariff barrier nexus is presented in an UNCTAD study of chemical fibres, summarized in Table 3.6.

Foreign investment of this type extends abroad to exploit the firms own competitive edge in capital, technical know-how regardless of the comparative advantage of the host country and has therefore been characterized as being 'anti-trade oriented' (Kojima, 1975). It feeds on and fuels market compartmentalization. The thrust of foreign investment in LDCs has hitherto been of this sort; it concentrates in sectors in which barriers to the entry of native producers are among the highest, i.e. in industries with oligopolistic features (Dunning, 1970; Hymer, 1976; Vernon, 1971). On the other hand, LDCs have been keen to attract such firms precisely because of the resources and sophisticated technology in their hands.

Table 3.6 Great Britain and Pakistan: comparative polyester costs, 1976

	UK producer		National Fibres Ltd. of Pakistan	
	US cents/lb	per cent	US cents/lb	per cent
Raw material	31.36	56.0	47.35	55.0
Labour	7.84	14.0	1.30	1.5
Services, energy etc.	5.60	10.0	7.29	8.5
Maintenance	2.24	4.0	0.32	0.3
Depreciation	3.36	6.0	10.50	12.2
Capital costs	5.60	10.0	19.40	22.5
Total manufacturing costs	56.00	100.0	86.16	100.0
Sales and distribution costs	18.00		2.64*	
Total costs	74.0		88.80	

* Does not include transportation costs.

Source: International Trade Centre, UNCTAD/GATT, 'Marketing of Pakistan Polyester Products in International Markets', March 1977, in UNCTAD, *Textiles and Fibres: Dimensions of Corporate Structure* (1980).

In Latin America the encouragement of such investment was an integral part of import substitution programmes. Peter B. Evans's study of the relationship between the Brazilian state and MNCs noted that the development of the petrochemical sector the participation of MNCs in the project was crucial to Petroquisa, the Brazilian state-owned enterprise. Technology is, of course, one of the multinationals' prime contributions.

It would have been possible to purchase most of the technology, but buying technology has disadvantages. An engineering firm does not have the same interest in future profits that a partner does. Once a plant is constructed the engineers are not there to deal with the problems ... Petroquisa was looking for full, continuous access to the most advanced technology available, taking on multi-national partners was the best way to get it. [P. B. Evans, 1979, p. 192.]

Once established, these firms' attitudes to trade will not differ from native firms. They will have a vested interest in protection from imports and will not naturally be inclined to seek export markets. David Morawetz's study of the Colombian synthetic fibre industry underlined the fact that such plants, whether locally- or foreign-owned, were able to survive only because they received substantial protection against foreign competition from the government's tariff and licensing system. Four of the five synthetic fibre plants so protected are more than 50 per cent foreign-owned (Morawetz, 1982, p. 92). Obviously, Colombian synthetic fibres, priced well above world levels, are rarely exported.

Given uncompetitiveness in world markets, only extensive state intervention and incentives will lead to exports. For example, UNCTAD notes that in petrochemicals Mexico's state petroleum enterprise (PEMEX) offered private companies a 30 per cent discount on raw mateials, fuel and electricity. In return, the companies were expected to sell part of their output abroad, 'a provision designed to enlist the global marketing capabilities of the petrochemical conglomerates' (UNCTAD, *Fibres* ..., 1980, p. 116). In Brazil the corporations have been stimulated by tax concessions, including the elimination of corporate income tax; the abolition of sales and other taxes, amounting to 15 to 18 per cent of product value. According to ECLA, of every dollar's-worth of textile products exported from Brazil, 71 cents represented subsidies, and of every 100 million dollars' worth of vehicles exported, 66 million were subsidies granted to the sector (ECLA, *Economic Survey*, 1980, p. 119.)

The anti-export orientation of such investments is also reflected in the relative lack of interest in Latin America's regional market. The evidence seems to suggest that few firms changed their anti-export orientation with the creation of the Latin American Free Trade Area. Most firms, whether national or international, remained defensive of their import substitution pattern of investment and failed to provide an impetus for regional trade liberalization. Having begun their business to substitute for imports and having replicated their investments throughout the region, they remained primarily bound to the national market. The extension of parallel production facilities meant that rationalization required sizeable financial and management resources. One UNCTAD study, from which it is worth quoting in full, reports:

> A frank and precise summary of the attitudes of such firms towards economic integration was given in an interview by the top manager of one of the largest foreign automobile subsidiaries in Mexico. He said: 'It might make a lot of economic sense in the long run to merge our operations in the region and to introduce some degree of intra-firm specialization in respect of final products, parts and accessories instead of working for a dozen individual markets absorbing annually from 10,000 to 130,000 each. But such operations would involve complete overhaul of our productive assembly facilities and an outlay of perhaps several hundred million dollars ... There is little reason for us to engage in such gigantic financial and technological operations as long as we can get fairly satisfactory profits from actual investments with small additional capital outlays and technological adjustments geared to the slow growth of individual domestic markets.' [UNCTAD, 1982, *The Role* . . . , p. 6.]

3.5 INTERNATIONALIZATION OF COMPARATIVE ADVANTAGE BY INTERNATIONAL FIRMS

International capital is not homogeneous in nature. Some firms are interested in free trade, some are not. The role of international firms as generators of freer international trade will differ according to whether investments have aimed at exploiting company-specific monopolistic advantages (arcane technology, finance, etc.) or exploiting the comparative advantages of the host country. When a firm sets up an operation abroad to take advantage of lower relative costs in the host country, it internalizes the comparative advantage, i.e. the country's facilities become incorporated into the global network of specialization of the firm. The firm will become a push–pull factor towards more and freer trade. Then, 'Trade and investment, far from being alternative forms of international involvement, are one and the same thing. More precisely, foreign "investment" is trade of a particular type: internalised trade' (Vaitsos, 1980, p. 31).

In such cases MNCs develop an integrated strategy for world-wide production and sales and therefore, in fact, promote an international division of labour internal to their own organizations. Resources are deployed among the branches in different countries specializing in the production of components which are then transferred across national boundaries for the assemby of the final good. Successive stages in the chain of production of one article can take place in several countries so that a sizeable, though difficult to estimate, part of the growth of international trade is in effect the growth of intra-firm transfers. Internationally decentralized firms are naturally keen to establish and maintain free international exchanges for the inputs and components which they require and which they produce and trade internationally. Where intra-firm arrangements exist, protection is, at the very least, an inconvenience to the firm and therefore firms will support freer trade rather than protection. 'Internalised trade assures smooth and reliable exchanges.' (Vaitsos, 1980, p. 33).

Intra-firm shipments are especially prominent in the production and trade of computers. Some of the phases of production of the Apple computer, whose international itinerary was traced above (*The Guardian*, op. cit.), are in effect intra-firm shipments: for example, the company in Singapore is owned by Apple. *The Economist*, in underlining the extent up to which IBM has decentralized its operations, noted that:

> IBM would lose more than any Japanese computer company from barriers in the west against exports of Japanese computers and computer parts: Japanese officials reckon that shipments of IBM Japan to other parts of the company account for one-third of the value of Japan's computer exports. [*The Economist*, 19 February 1983, p. 85.]

On the other hand, five Japanese companies have opened plants in the United States, so in 1981 Japan and the United States were able to agree on a reciprocal tariff reduction on semiconductors (which includes computer memory chips) to a nominal 4.2 per cent from April 1982, six years in advance of the timetable negotiated during the Tokyo Round (IMF, 1982, p. 29). In 1985 a further reduction was agreed which brought the import duty to zero in both countries. Since, for such firms, protection is a cost, the computer market will tend in comparison to be less conflict-prone than other relatively less internationally decentralized sectors such as motor cars or video cassette recorders, where rivalry among firms is more likely to lead to inter-governmental conflict with more ease. For instance, a conflict between British Leyland and Ford over tariff differentials between Britain and Spain almost automatically became an inter-governmental trade dispute between Britain and Spain (*The Financial Times*, 28 February 1983 and 5 March 1983). A dispute between the EEC and Japan on exports of video cassette recorders to the EEC was similarly a result of pressures by Philips and Grundig. When Japan agreed to limit exports, *The Financial Times* noted that for the EEC 'a central objective is to protect Philips of Holland and Grundig of West Germany by giving them a guaranteed market share and sheltering them from price competition' (*The Financial Times*, 21 February 1983). Since the Japanese agreed to align their prices with European manufactures, 'Philips and Grundig will in effect set the price which the Japanese, the most efficient producers, will charge' (*The Financial Times*, 15 February 1983).

This particular pattern of internationalization of capital has hitherto mainly been manifest among industrialized countries. Evidence of this can be extracted from the evolution of intra-firm transfers assessed by Helleiner (1981) which covers only the 1966–75 period and imports into the United States originating in American business abroad. This is naturally only a part of the picture; nevertheless, the leading role of the American economy warrants some safe generalizations if only as an indicator of the trend. One-third of total American imports are sales of foreign affiliates of American parent firms. While the share of American non-oil imports from LDCs that originates in American multinationals abroad has declined, the equivalent share from Western Europe and Canada has increased.[7] At the beginning of the period under study, intra-firm trade made up 20 per cent of American non-oil imports from LDCs; in 1975 it accounted for only 11 per cent. It seems that vertically integrated transnational enterprises are only responsible for a minor and declining share of LDCs' exports to the United States. Helleiner concludes that, at least as far as American-based firms are concerned, the internationalization and vertical integration of production is mainly confined to the North Atlantic, while the share of American non-oil imports from LDCs which originates in MNCs is decreasing. Helleiner attributes this decline to two factors, one of which is the increasing involvement of state-trading companies in primary commodities. But the factor of relevance to our discussion is the changing composition of LDCs' exports: a growing share of them consists of manufactures, trade in which is typically less subject to management by foreign firms than is primary commodity trade (Helleiner, 1981). The exception to this trend is the offshore assembly of goods, which will be discussed below. Obviously, at a less aggregate level, there are differences from country to country, with a broad spectrum ranging from Singapore, where 70 per cent of exports are handled by MNCs, to Brazil's 40 per cent and India's low of 5 per cent (Perry, 1982, p. 138).

3.5.1 Offshore assembly of goods

An exception to this concentration of intra-industry and intra-firm trade among developed countries is offshore assemby of goods in LDCs. Offshore assembly is an arrangement whereby a firm contracts abroad the processing or assembly of a product, or component manufacturing. It involves the geographical relocation of the labour-intensive stages of fabrication of an article to take advantage of lower wage costs in labour-rich countries. This phase of production may be delegated to a foreign subsidiary of the parent company or may be subcontracted to an unrelated foreign party. The first instance is a case of capital export and intra-firm trade; in the latter there is intra-industry trade, whereby two different firms establish a contractual relationship with no necessary equity links.

Such assembly for re-export of components originating in industrialized countries constitutes a rapidly growing part of the manufactured exports of some LDCs. A study by Finger (1975) noted that this activity is encouraged by the existence of provisions in the tariff structure of nearly all industrial countries which give duty-free re-entry to domestically produced components which have been assembled abroad. The tariff is only applied to the value added in the assembly process, if domestically produced components are used.

In 1964 the United States enacted two tariff provisions to foster these activities: tariff items 807.00 and 806.30. While tariff item 806.30 covers offshore processing of certain metal products which are then returned to the United States for further processing, tariff item 807.00 refers to manufactured goods. It indicates that:

> Articles assembled abroad in whole or in part of fabricated components, the product of the United States, which (a) were exported in condition ready for assembly without further fabrication; (b) have not lost their physical identity in such articles by change in form, shape, or otherwise, and (c) have not been advanced in value or improved in condition abroad except by being assembled and except by operations incidental to the assembly ·process such as cleaning, lubricating, and painting. [US, International Trade Commission,1978, p. 29.]

Whether it is intra-firm trade or merely intra-industry trade (unrelated parties within the same industrial branch), both trends are a way of internalizing the lower costs offered by more labour-rich countries within the manufacturing operations of firms in industrialized countries. Helleiner's study reports that offshore assembly has grown at rates considerably in excess of the rates of growth in total American manufacturing imports. LDCs' exports under this tariff provision have also grown more rapidly than their total manufacturing exports to the United States. By 1975 (a decade after the enactment of the tariff provisions) this trade made up 15 per cent of total manufactured imports from developing countries. Most American imports under this tariff provision are electronic components (Table 3.7). Mexico has accounted for the largest share of these imports, followed by Taiwan, Singapore, Hong Kong and Malaysia.

Parallel with the making of these tariff provisions in the United States, Mexico instituted its 'maquila' or border industrialization programme to attract American firms to relocate production in assembly sites just inside the border. Electrical motors and equipment, semi-conductors and parts and

Table 3.7 Industry distribution of offshore assembled products, 1972 (%)

Industry	United States		Netherlands		West Germany
	From all countries	From developing countries	From all countries	From Eastern Europe	From all countries
Processed foods, beverages	—	—	1	—	1
Chemicals, rubber, plastic materials	—	—	4	—	2
Textile products	3	8	41	95	49
Electronic products	18	56	—	—	—
Machinery	27	13	29	—	29
Motor vehicles, including aircraft	39	—	4	—	6
Scientific precision instruments	1	2	5	—	2
Misc. metal products	9	11	9	—	3
Other manufactures	3	10	7	5	8

Source: Finger (1975).

television receivers, where foreign firms were prominent, accounted for 44 per cent of total *maquila* exports. In contrast, made-up clothing, a much more labour-intensive product, accounted for only 9 per cent of border exports. Moreover, apparel factories 'typically were smaller and possessed a larger proportion of Mexican capital investment.' (Dillman, 1983, p. 44).

The different contribution to exports of these border industries is largely a function of their respective ownership patterns. Both export performance and ownership are connected to the behaviour of American companies in these sectors. These corporate decisions are not only reflected in Mexico's *maquila* exports, but also in American imports under tariff provision 807.00, as shown in Table 3.7. Whereas the electrical and electronic companies have shifted investments abroad, and especially to the Mexican border and South Asian countries, the textiles and clothing firms have relocated production within the United States itself from the higher-wage areas of the north-east to the lower-wage areas of the south, where a significant proportion of labour is un-unionized, of Hispanic origin and frequently illegal (Pelzman, 1982). This means that firms can combine low wages within the United States itself with the advantages of the more sophisticated infrastructure (communications, transport, etc.) that the country can offer, together with closer proximity to consumers. This is of crucial importance for the small firms that typically operate in this sector. Two-thirds of American textile firms have less than fifty employees (*South*, August 1983, p. 61).

Two other developed countries where trade flows under these value-added tariff provisions have experienced buoyant growth are West Germany and the Netherlands. There, to be eligible for value-added tariffs, the imported products must be made from components exported by a domestic enterprise on its own account; they must be processed abroad on the account of that enterprise; and they must be imported by that enterprise on its own account (Finger, 1975, p. 365). Whereas in the United States value-added tariff provisions were mainly used by the electronics companies, in the Netherlands and West Germany most value-added imports are textile products (see Table 3.7) originating mainly in Eastern Europe and more recently in the Mediterranean countries (Joekes, 1982).

With offshore assembly, LDCs become increasingly integrated into trade-orientated investment flows, if only as appendages of foreign manufacture. The different performance of the Mexican border industries shows that, for the value-adding LDCs, a policy of promoting offshore processing is not in itself a sufficient incentive to attract labour-intensive processes on an even keel. Some processes will be relocated, others are less likely to be, depending on corporate decisions that lie beyond the control of the processing country. Other limitations are placed on the processing country. It must use components from the country for which the assignment is being carried out. The exclusion of local components means that a supplying industry will not develop; no backward linkages will be fostered. Moreover, offshore assembly is normally exempt from local taxes and as a foreign exchange earner it is limited to the processing stage.

To be sure, from a more circumscribed commercial perspective, value-added tariffs and offshore assembly will allow the low-wage, labour-surplus countries to create employment and to perform the parts of a production process for which they enjoy so large an advantage. Corporate backing smoothes the obstacles to the integration of such cost differentials into international trade.

3.6 IMPLICATIONS

To recapitulate, 64 per cent of world trade in manufactures consists of chemical and engineering goods (see Table 3.4)—goods with low labour or raw material input in relation to capital. The production of such goods is less tied to either of the fixed factors of production—land and labour.

Trade has mostly flourished in capital-intensive goods, alongside four closely related trends. Firstly, 80 per cent of world trade and two-thirds of international investment concentrated in the developed countries. Secondly, the intra-industry trade of these international investors is a result of and results in industrial convergence; this is reflected in partial country specialization within industrial sectors rather than complete specialization, consequently obviating the pains of adjustment. The process has been facilitated by the increasing technological development of products leading to product differentiation and the decline of price competition relative to quality or model competition. Firms and countries have been able to carve out market niches owing more and more to the strength of the type of good produced rather than to its price. Thirdly, the market had become increasingly concentrated under the direction provided by the network of international investments which resulted from the mobility of capital between countries. Fourthly, some international specialization has been promoted within firms, leading to intra-firm trade.

At the intersection of these four trends is the multinational corporation which, having organized and internationalized production, was able to order and galvanize trade. Multinational corporations influenced the direction and commodity composition of international trade flows. There is, to the author's knowledge, no systematic tally of the value of world trade in manufactures attributed to all MNCs. One estimate ventured by UNCTAD is that about two-thirds of all international trade can be attributed to MNCs (*Trade and Development Report*, 1981, p. 64). Although international investment did flow to LDCs, they remained at the margin of the trends described above. As was noted above, a considerable part of international investment in LDCs, industrial sector was undertaken regardless of efficiency and thus its output did not flow naturally into international trade, but required the active involvement of the state in the way of direct subsidies, tax exemptions, etc. Such higher-cost facilities could not easily become export-orientated, if at all. More importantly, trade between developed countries and LDCs, and among LDCs, remains largely based on inter-industrial specialization; their economies remained rivals rather than becoming interdependent through intra-industrial trade.

In any case, LDCs, not being major investing countries themselves, could not use their own capital exports for barrier jumping purposes, i.e. they could not use investment as an alternative to the export of goods when these were menaced. This is a technique that has become widely used by Japanese companies. Nissan, for example, threatened by the imposition of trade restrictions on truck exports to the United States, responded by announcing that it would set up a local plant to make ten thousand trucks a month from 1983. Nissan's executive vice-president was quoted as saying, 'It would be a lie if I deny there is a relationship to the US tariff' (*Fortune*, 11 August 1980, p. 108). This technique was described by the same source as 'our strategy of internationalisation to improve access to crucial foreign markets.'[8]

Internationalization of capital has, moreover, played a central role in integrating investing countries ever more closely. There are several facets to this close integration and consequent mutuality of interests. One of these is exemplified by the case of the British subsidiary of the Japanese company Sony which received the Queen's Award for Export, with its Japanese manager receiving the Order of the British Empire (Cable, 1983). A more advanced stage of mutuality of interests is the case mentioned above, of an accelerated pace of reciprocal tariff reductions in semiconductors by Japan and the United States, following their reciprocal investments. Lastly, internationalized enterprises can and do enter into joint ventures, thus softening rivalry. Among many examples, ICI, Britain's largest chemical group, has been involved in a joint venture with the American Celanese Corporation to produce polyester yarn in the United States (*The Financial Times*, 26 May 1983). Hercules, a leading American chemical company, and Montedison of Italy, two of the world's leading manufacturers of polypropylene resins, are to combine their businesses in a world-wide joint venture company which will involve their plants in the United States, Canada, Italy and Belgium. 'In addition', *The Financial Times* reported, 'the deal will give Hercules access to advanced new technology developed by Montedison in conjunction with Mitsui of Japan' (18 May 1983). Such close business ties will blur the nationality of capital and should tend to reduce conflicts. An element of market sharing is intrinsic to such operations. In turn, the propensity of states to get involved in trade disputes should decline, given the interest of all actors involved in maintaining the freedom for such international exchanges. No such possibilities are available to LDCs at the receiving ends of capital movements.

The international market consequently follows the pattern that results from the particular combination of liberalization and protection. This pattern is imprinted by the direction of capital flows and the freer mobility of capital relative to other factors of production. While capital-intensive goods have experienced greater trade growth and greater tariff reductions, the exchange of labour-intensive goods remains relatively protected, with below-average tariff reductions as well as a greater incidence of non-tariff regulations. The average tariff rate of industrialized countries on industrial products was 10.6 per cent prior to the Tokyo Round and will be reduced to 6.5 per cent as a result of the negotiations (GATT, 1979, p. 120). Within this average, tariffs on processed goods escalate according to the degree of processing, that is as the labour-intensity of production increases (Table 3.8).

This escalation of the tariff as one moves from primary to the first stages of processing activities can be interpreted as a reflection of the need for the raw material caused by the absence of local production. Without such imports, domestic manufacturing would be disrupted. But, for the further stages of processing, another explanation is required. Helleiner associates above-average rates of protection in labour-intensive products with the absence of MNC interest in such products. MNCs use their political power to press vigorously, 'for trade barrier reduction in those commodity classifications in

Table 3.8 Tariff barriers according to degree of processing of selected products in eleven major DCs (%)

Products	Average tariff rates
Iron	
Iron ore	0
Unwrought iron	2.4
Iron and steel plates	9.3
Knives, forks, etc.	18.8
Aluminium	
Bauxite	0
Oxide	3.9
Plates	5.4
Foil	12.8
Rubber	
Rubber	0.1
Tyres	9.3
Rubber footwear	16.5
Leather	
Hides and skins	9.6
Suitcases	13.1
Footwear	16.4
Wood	
Timber	0
Sawn wood	2.2
Chairs, etc.	11.5
Plywood	16.7
Textiles	
Cotton, not carded or combed	1.1
Carded and combed cotton	5.2
Cotton textiles	8.2
Knitted cotton	12.4
Men's and children's clothing	23.1
Knitted clothing	26.9

Source: World Bank, 'Trade Liberalization and Export Promotion', in G. Perry, 1982, p. 136.

which they themselves trade, and show no particular interest in those relatively labour-intensive industries in which they are not directly involved' (Helleiner, 1981. p. 82). Helleiner concluded that the result is a bias in trade barriers against products not traded by MNCs.

This chapter has argued similarly that there is such a bias, though not merely because of the political power of MNCs. Such an explanation would have the ring of conspiracy theory. The argument made in this chapter is that trade expansion cannot be understood separately from the pattern of international investments which concentrated in the developed countries and in capital-intensive sectors. Such investments not only acted as generators of trade, they also provided an order in which the patterns of trade and investment followed each other.

A point that has hitherto only been hinted at, and that can also provide an explanation for the escalation of tariffs as processing advances, is that, since the war, developed countries have tended to take into account in the elaboration of trade policies the need to keep unemployment to a minimum— a point acknowledged in the GATT preamble[9] as well as in Article XII.

One need only look at the vast disparity in labour costs between developed markets and LDCs (Figure 3.1)[10] to understand W. Arthur Lewis's point that:

> developed countries have gone to extremes to keep out manufactures from the developing countries, for exactly the same reasons that they have kept out Asian migrants. They have imported raw produce, but have placed heavy import duties or prohibitions on refined produce in order to protect their own manufacturing capacity. [Lewis, 1977, p. 32.]

Developed countries wishing to protect employment will be under pressure to restrict the inflow of lower-priced, labour-intensive goods. The pressure for protection will be greater the more labour-intensive and the less skill-intensive the industry, since labour costs as a share of total costs form a greater part of such goods.[11] Because of the extreme wage differentials—for example, South Korea's labour costs in the textile industry are a mere 12 per cent of West Germany's (Figure 3.1)—labour-intensive goods will be produced more efficiently by LDCs and imports of such goods will tend to displace employment in developed countries. What is more, imports will have an impact on the least qualified workers and the more depressed areas. If imports of such goods absorb an increasing share of the market, that particular industrial sector in the importing country will be forced to contract; production will shift to the country with lower relative wages. Such wide disparities of relative costs and the attendant risk of displacement are precisely the reason for protectionism. And protectionism aimed at arresting the pressure of wage competition is part and parcel of full employment and welfare policies. For capital-intensive goods, as we have seen, no such relocation is required as market niches were captured, firstly, on quality and differentiation and only secondly on lower prices.

Regulations preventing mass migrations from labour surplus countries and the consequent development of an international labour market must, of necessity, be accompanied by regulations to restrict the inflow of the goods produced by those so restricted. The escalation of the tariff of developed countries by stages of production indicates the extent to which the tariff permits labour costs in the country's industry to exceed the value of labour's contribution at world market prices. Myrdal was among the first to stress that

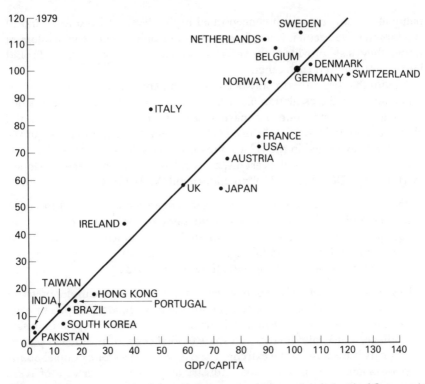

Figure 3.1 Labour costs in the textile industry and income levels (as % of Germany)
Source: Gesamtextil, Comitextil, UN Monthly Bulletin.

labour mobility 'would make for greater flexibility in the whole industrial system and create possibilities for freer trade' (Myrdal, 1956, p. 96). Though he also realistically acknowledged that labour migration was not without its problems: 'To ask the richer countries to open up their boundaries to mass immigration from the poor countries, which have not solved their population problem, would, indeed, be very questionable international idealism' (Myrdal, 1956, p. 95).

This matter is not only a force conspiring against LDCs' exports to the developed countries; it must of necessity also bear on South–South trade since LDCs are obviously equally concerned with protecting their own employment and will not wish to import competing labour-intensive products from each other. More generally, given that LDC trade is still of the traditional inter-industry rather than of the intra-industry type, their econ-omies have not developed into the sort of interdependence that draws developed countries together. Centrifugal forces still prevail among LDCs as they do between LDCs and developed countries.

The broad trends reviewed in this chapter have offered a description of the present character of world commerce, including the part played by LDCs. The implications for them will be pointed up more sharply in subsequent pages in which this constellation of factors will be seen at play, firstly in a South–North direction and, secondly, in a South–South direction.

NOTES

1. In 1985 this typical pattern in which the growth of trade exceeds the growth of production was interrupted for the first time in the post-war period.
2. My thanks to Michael Banks for drawing my attention to this piece.
3. This type of intra-trade is known as vertical intra-industry specialization (where different parts, components, or raw materials are shipped to produce the final good), in contrast to the horizontal intra-industry specialization in differentiated final goods, for example Apple computers for Sinclair or Citroens for Austins.
4. Strange and Tooze's (1981) selection of industrial sectors with surplus capacity would support this point.
5. This decline in LDCs' share was especially attributable to the geographical redistribution of American private investment. While in 1950 American foreign investment was more or less equally distributed between developed and developing areas, with roughly one half in each, by 1980 the shares of each had changed drastically, with 70 per cent for developed and 30 per cent for LDCs countries (Griffith-Jones, 1983).
6. In Chapter 6 we shall see how this structure of investment was a factor that worked against regional integration in Latin America.
7. For further insight into the investment and trade pattern: American-owned multi-national corporations in Europe accounted for 12 per cent of total American imports from Europe, 55 per cent for Canada and 1 per cent for Japan (Helleiner, 1981).
8. There is evidence that LDCs may be following this pattern precisely in the sectors in which they have become substantial exporters and in which they are faced with trade restrictions; for example two of Hong Kong's knitwear companies have set up a factory in the North of England and in Ireland, a Brazilian steel company in California etc.
9. 'Recognizing that their relations in the field of trade and economic endeavour should be conducted with a view to raising standards of living, ensuring full employment . . .'
10. My thanks to Ebba Dohlman for this figure.
11. Research by David S. Ball for the United States found a positive correlation between the level of effective protection and unskilled labour intensity (1967). See also Basevi (1966), Balassa (1965), as well as documents for UNCTAD I (UNCTAD, E. Conf. 46/PC/20, 6 May 1963).

4 The Multifibre Agreement: origins and consequences

4.1 INTRODUCTION

The true nature of international trade being as I have indicated in the preceding chapter, and not the GATT myth, I am now going to show how in two ways LDCs accommodated themselves to this true nature. In the present chapter I will take a sectoral approach and look at the exports of textiles of all LDCs taken together. In the following chapter I will move away from the sectoral orientation to take a regional one and concentrate on the Latin American Free Trade Association.

Since the late 1950s the United States and Europe have been seeking ways of establishing the flow of imports of textiles and clothing, first from Japan and subsequently from the LDCs. In 1961, a one-year, Short-Term arrangement (STA) was drawn up under GATT auspices. It was then replacd by a four-year Long-Term Arrangement (LTA) in 1962. The LTA was signed by the governments of nineteen exporting and importing countries and was subsequently renewed in 1967 and 1970. In 1974 it was replaced by the Multi-Fibre Arrangement (MFA), twice renewed since then. These agreements, though sanctioned by GATT, are a derogation from its rules since they impose a system of quota control of South–North textile trade over and above the MFN tariff rates. The quota system is specified by country of origin, country of destination and product categories. Moreover, although the STA, the LTA and the MFA provided a framework for negotiations, the quotas themselves are agreed on a bilateral basis, thus also violating the GATT principle of non-discrimination. The existence of the MFA and its precursors has thus led to a situation in which trade in the textile sector follows principles totally opposed to those for which the GATT stood.

4.2 FEATURES OF THE AGREEMENT

The MFA , like the LTA before it, is essentially an umbrella that covers quota agreements negotiated bilaterally between an exporting and an importing country. For example, under the MFA the United States has bilaterals with twenty-one countries covering 107 product categories; the ECC has twenty-five bilaterals, covering 123 product categories. The agreements specify the conditions under which an export restraint can be requested or under which a quantitative restriction can be imposed unilaterally. Both the MFA and the LTA were devised as a compromise whereby, in exchange for a guaranteed expansion of their exports, LDCs agreed to exercise self-restraint and (*de facto* if not *de jure*) to waive their other rights under GATT, such as Article XIII (Non-discrimination in the Administration of Quantitative Restrictions) and therefore also in part the right of retaliation (Article XXIII) and the right to compensatory concession (Article XIX on Safeguard Procedures). In the years before the conclusion of the LTA, several exporting countries had been approached by importers with requests to limit their exports. In 1956 the United States had asked Japan to restrict her exports. In 1959 industry-to-industry quotas had been agreed between Great Britain, Hong Kong, India and Pakistan. To these leading export-orientated Asian countries, multi-lateralization seemed preferable to strictly bilateral agreements. Besides the promise that there would be yearly increases in their quotas, the LTA guaranteed that other exporting countries would also be bound by the regulations (Article 6.c) so that the space left by self-restriction could not be occupied by a newcomer. Moreover, it stipulated the levels of trade on which quotas could be applied and offered the promise of multilateral supervision. It did indeed seem, as the Preamble of the LTA said, the convenient regulatory vehicle:

> to provide growing opportunities for exports of these products, provided that the development of this trade proceeds in a reasonable and orderly manner so as to avoid disruptive effects in individual markets or in individual lines of production in both importing and exporting countries [LTA, Preamble.]

The condition on the basis of which controls could be imposed was that exports by a given country were 'causing or tending to cause market disruption' (Article 3).

The limitations of the LTA applied only to cotton products, not to raw cotton. It covered yarns, piece goods, made-up articles, garments and other textile-manufactured production in which cotton was 50 per cent or more of fibre content by weight, with the exception of hand-loomed products of the cottage industries (Article 9). It was initially signed by nineteen countries and covered the five-year period from 1962 to 1967. It was renewed in 1967 and again in 1970. By 1973, when it was due to expire, there were eighty-three signatories. The LTA had stipulated that measures under its aegis, 'are intended to deal with the special problem of cotton textiles, and they are not to be considered as lending themselves to application in other fields' (Article 1). But by the early 1970s a major industrial change had occurred.

Alongside a shift from cotton to man-made fibres, the industry was transformed into a multi-fibre industry with traditional barriers between processes and fibres becoming increasingly blurred. Besides, the restraint on cotton exports had created an incentive for exporting countries to shift to non-restricted fibres. For example, while imports of cotton textiles to the United States doubled from 1960 to 1970, imports of man-made fibre textiles grew more than tenfold (US, International Trade Commission, 1978, p. vi).

In 1971 the United States succeeded in signing export restraint agreements with five Asian countries, covering wool and man-made fibres in addition to cotton products. Pressure to widen the scope of this system of controls gathered momentum, and during 1973 negotiations were opened to devise a more comprehensive coverage extending to the whole textile industry. Thus the MFA came into effect in January 1974 for an initial period of four years. Article 2 declares the objectives of the MFA to be:

> to achieve the expansion of trade, the reduction of barriers to such trade and the progressive liberalisation of world trade in textile products, while at the same time ensuring the orderly and equitable development of this trade and avoidance of disruptive effects in individual markets and on individual lines of production in both importing and exporting countries.

Two types of restrictions are envisaged: in the first place, the tighter ones under Article 3 which permit controls as a result of market disruption; in the second place, those under Article 4 which permit bilateral agreements 'to eliminate real risks of market disruption in the importing countries'. Article 3 restrictions can be imposed either by negotiation or unilaterally. The provision for unilateral action is the ultimate safeguard for importing countries. It can be used on an emergency basis or when negotiations break down—thus ensuring that the exporting country cannot frustrate protectionist measures merely by stalling in negotiations. This Article 'should only be resorted to sparingly and its application shall be limited to the precise products and to countries whose exports of such products are causing market disruption'. Article 4 can be invoked more easily because only 'risk of market disruption' need exist, but 'bilateral agreements maintained under this Article shall, on overall terms, including base levels and growth rates, be more liberal'. Normally, base levels and growth rates are fixed on the criterion of past performance but Article 6.2 recognizes that new entrants should be accorded special treatment and their past performance not be taken into account. Article 6.3 stipulates that quotas on small suppliers should be avoided.

These provisions offered an initial incentive for participation to the LDCs whose exports lagged behind and hoped to catch up with a dynamic export growth of the South-east Asian countries. The restraints on the latter, coupled with special considerations for the less competitive, meant that they had access to a guaranteed market share from the very start. In practice, it seems that the system has not totally delivered the promise. The EEC, the United States and Canada have negotiated bilaterals with countries supplying less than 1 per cent of the market or even with no imports recorded (UNCTAD/MTN/CB.22, 1980). Even limited market presence can attract a quota.

In 1977 the MFA was renewed to cover a further four-year period, from 1978 to 1982. At the insistence of the European Community, the Protocol of Extension included a clause allowing 'jointly agreed reasonable departures' from particular provisions of the agreement (paragraph 5.3). This clause gave the EEC license to negotiate bilateral agreements that were more restrictive in terms of import growth than in the first four years of the MFA. Imports of products considered 'sensitive' were restricted to an annual growth of 0.2 per cent. The reasonable departures clause also applied to the provisions of the MFA contained in Annexe B regulating 'flexibility' in the use of quotas, i.e. the provisions that allowed and regulated switching between product categories (a procedure known as 'swing' in the jargon), use of an unfulfilled quota from the preceding year ('carry over'), or advance use of some of the following year's quota ('carry forward'). As a result, imports from MFA signatories grew by 54 per cent in value from 1977 to 1979 while imports from non-restricted sources grew by 63 per cent. For example, while imports into the EEC from Hong Kong, Taiwan and South Korea increased by 55, 43 and 42 per cent respectively, imports from Portugal grew by 105 per cent (US, International Trade Commission, 1983, p. 135).

The third renegotiation took place in 1981. The reasonable departures clause was dropped but two further major restrictions were introduced in the Protocol Extension. In the first place, the growth rate of the market was introduced as a new element to determine the allowed import growth of a given country. The measure was aimed at holding the import share of the market constant so that domestic and foreign suppliers were obliged to share the growth of demand in the same proportion as given by their initial positions. The second innovation was the inclusion of a clause which could be used to curtail the growth of exports within a given quota that so far has remained unfulfilled. This, in effect, implied that even an allocated quota would not be a full guarantee that the corresponding market share would be made available. The rigidity of the scheme was further enhanced by provisions for consultations to avoid greatly increased imports, either in categories or from countries without specified quotas.

The story was re-enacted yet again when the 1981 extension was due to expire. In 1986 the United States demanded that made-up goods of hitherto unrestricted natural fibres, such as silk, ramie, jute, coir, sisal, abaca, maguey and henequen, be brought under the MFA umbrella. It was argued that unprecedently large increments in imports using these fibres were disrupting the Americn market and additional coverage was consequently required. The

1986 MFA thus extended its coverage to restrain these fibres as well. But there was more than that: it was renewed for five years instead of the usual four.

The United States, besides its twenty-two bilaterals, has agreements with ten other countries which provide 'for discussions of possible limitations when problems arise' (US, International Trade Commission, 1978, p. vii), i.e. an import threshold per country and per product category is established which, once reached, can trigger a consultation procedure aimed at forestalling further import growth. The EEC has had four agreements providing for consultation in addition to its twenty-five bilaterals with specific category limitations.

4.3 THE CONCEPT OF MARKET DISRUPTION

Protectionist policies in the textile and clothing industries were not born suddenly in the 1960s but what was novel was the creation of a global regulatory framework to oversee trade flows in a specific direction from low to high-cost countries. The study by Alfred Maizels, *Industrial Growth and World Trade*, shows evidence that tariff protection of textiles and clothing in 1937 was higher than the average for manufactured goods in both high and low-tariff industrialized countries (Maizels, 1963, p. 179). In the United States the Tariff Acts of 1922 and 1930 guaranteed for this sector higher levels of tariff protection than for most other manufactures and yet Japan—a lower-wage country—was still perceived to be a threat needing more effective means of control. To that end, in 1935, what seems to be the first 'voluntary export quota' was negotiated between the two countries (Destler, 1979, pp. 28–9).

After the war, textile and clothing trade in Europe was gradually liberalized within the framework of the Organization for European Economic Co-operation in the early 1950s, but restrictions against other non-European countries were retained under GATT Article XII which permits restraints to safeguard the balance of payments. When the major European currencies reached full external convertibility in 1958, recourse to Article XII was no longer justified. Yet Japan had acceded to the GATT three years before, and there was widespread apprehension about the impressive regrowth of Japanese manufactured exports. Keesing and Wolf (1980) note that in 1959 when Japan was the world's leading textile exporter she had merely regained the 19 per cent share of world exports which she had achieved in 1937.

In 1960 the French government declared in GATT that 'a country in the course of technical modernisation or industrialisation is likely to benefit for a certain time from a combination of modern techniques and a low standard of living' (in Curzon and Curzon, 1976, p. 253). The implication of this statement was that such particular circumstances merited derogation from GATT rules on equality of treatment.[1] Cost differentials *vis-à-vis* Japan meant that competition on equal grounds could no longer be sustained. This situation, as Dam points out, 'began to seem less like a specifically Japanese problem than like a generic problem of international trade in manufactures between countries with different levels of wages' (Dam, 1970, p. 297).[2] With the desire to protect themselves from more competitive goods, a makeshift concept emerged, 'market disruption'. The concept provided the rationale for a specific and systematic regulation of imports from such lower-wage countries to higher-wage countries.

In November 1959 the United States introduced on the GATT agenda a discussion of 'the question of market disruption due to sudden large growth of imports from low wage countries' (US, International Trade Commission, 1978, p. v). In the event a definition of the concept was worked out that specified that the following elements combined to create a situation of market disruption:

(i) a sharp and substantial increase or potential increase of imports of particular products from particular sources;
(ii) these products are offered at prices which are substantially lower than those prevailing for similar goods of comparable quality in the market of the importing country.

It also clarified that 'the price differentials referred to above do not arise from governmental intervention in the fixing or formation of prices or from dumping practices' and that this situation caused 'serious damage to domestic producers or threats thereof' (Decision of 19 November 1960, GATT, BISD, 9th S, 1961, p. 26; LTA, Annexe C; MFA, Annexe A). In sum, the concept referred to a situation in which imports were lower-priced relative to domestic goods, the implication being that trade could not be continued in such circumstances.

As Dam has sharply pointed out

This definition did not, it should be noted, refer to the causes of the exporting country's effectiveness in penetrating the domestic markets of the importing countries. There was no suggestion that the exporting country was doing anything improper. Rather, the principle of comparative advantage itself was being called into question . . . it became increasingly clear that there was but a difference in degree, not a difference in substance, between the conditions that gave rise to an ordinary increase in international trade and those that gave rise to the economic impact associated with the concept of market disruption. [Dam, 1970, p. 199.]

In essence, the concept was a contradiction in terms within free-trade philosophy. If it is assumed that the thrust of trade is the presence of comparative advantages, market disruption is a natural, even welcome, development as patterns of comparative advantages shift from country to

country, increasing global efficiency. 'Absolute stability is not only un-
obtainable but actually unwanted' (Blackhurst *et al.*, 1977, p. 258). In so far as
GATT was to provide the basis for the development of international trade
precisely on the basis of comparative advantage, the concept was spurious.
Yet because the thrust of world trade was no longer essentially based on price
competition, the notion was concocted to provide a cover for the textile
restrictions under LTA (Annexe C) and its heir the MFA (Annexe A). Both
LTA and MFA were conceived as regulatory vehicles to balances what for
GATT, in theory, ought to have been clashing objectives: guarding against
the disruption of markets while providing an opportunity for exports to grow.

At the instigation of the EEC, the Protocol of renewal of the third MFA in
1981 added a further criterion of market disruption. It was agreed that,
'decline in the rate of growth of per capita consumption in textiles and
clothing is an element which may be relevant to the recurrence or the exacer-
bation of a situation of market disruption' (paragraph 4). Thus, by implication, imports may not be growing at all but may nevertheless be disrupting
markets and thus be subject to tighter limitations. Market disruption has
become a euphemism for an inflexible system of preservation of historical
market shares irrespective of comparative costs.

4.4 SAFEGUARDS IN GATT

As argued in Chapter 3, post-war trade expansion had not required profound
adjustments to shifting patterns of comparative costs. This sort of shift occur-
ring in the textile sector was for GATT an unprecedented, though not unanticipated phenomenon. The consequences of free trade between unequal
economies is a long-standing subject of debate. In Latin America, and much
more massively in India, China and Egypt, handicraft industries had been
ruined by the onslaught of lower-cost manufactures from Western Europe in
the nineteenth century. Free trade had thus led to de-industrialization. In
Europe, List had noted that foreign trade produces

> better results between nations almost in the same degree of industrial
> advancement; between which, of course, competition, instead of being
> restrictive or paralyzing, and affording to one of the parties a monopoly, has
> only the effect, as in internal trade, of exciting emulation and stimulating
> improvements and reduction in prices [List, 1974, p. 403.]

He continued:

> Such is the case, for the most part, among the nations of the continent.
> France, Austria and the German Customs Union, for instance, might look
> for good results from the moderation in their duties, and even as between

those countries and Russia mutual concessions might be made for the common advantage. [List, 1974, p. 403.]

These problems had indeed received attention at the time of GATT's inception and it was thought that the institution would be equipped to cope with them in two ways. In the first place trade liberalization, rather than being forced by the stronger economies upon the weaker ones, would be a bargaining process. The GATT would provide a forum for equally sovereign governments to strike mutually advantageous bargains. The bargaining process would be governed only by supposedly impersonal sets of economic laws and political rules that applied equally to all countries. The weaker countries moreover, would have the benefits of international surveillance. Central to the system was the concept of non-discrimination. In this vision non-discrimination would protect small and weaker countries from the abuse of power by the large and strong ones

> There was to be no repetition of what was seen as a particular evil of the 1930s—the operation of bilateral bargaining through which a strong country, by the sheer use of its commercial power and, even more objectionably, its political power, imposed its own desired patterns of trade upon a weaker trading partner—no more cases of a Germany, in the manner of a Third Reich, forcing her East European neighbours to accept unwanted imports as payments for their exports, or of a Britain imposing clearing arrangements on Argentina to secure bilateral trade balance. [Golt, 1978, p. 10.]

The periodic tariff negotiations rounds would, moreover, allow accommodation to foreign competition to take place not on a once and for all basis but gradually. Among the classics, Adam Smith had sustained the notion that 'changes of this kind should never be introduced suddenly, but slowly, gradually, and after a long warning' [1776; 1976, p. 471) because 'equitable regard' was due to those producers affected by foreign competition.

A second device to mitigate the pains of accommodation should foreign competition prove excessively damaging to domestic producers, was GATT's main escape clause embodied in Article XIX. This article obviously reflected the expectation that reduction in trade barriers would be followed by geographical specialization. It was intended to provide a temporary shield to countries that find that as a result of tariff liberalization they are faced with the threat of extinction of affected sectors. It specifies that

> 'if, as a result of unforeseen developments and of the effect of the obligations incurred by a contracting party under this Agreement, including tariff concessions, any product is being imported into the territory of that contracting party in such increasing quantities and under such conditions as to cause or threaten serious injury to domestic producers ... the

contracting party shall be free, in respect of such product, and to the extent and for such time as may be necessary to prevent or remedy such injury, to suspend the obligation in whole or in part or to withdraw or modify the concessions. [General Agreement, paragraph 1(a).]

Given that the injury must be proved with reference to 'domestic producers of like or directly competitive products', the provision applies to the situation of countries with pre-existing domestic production. Safeguard action involves a defensive view of such production. It cannot be invoked to develop a novel product line. Hence it is natural that it has mostly been invoked by developed countries with established industries. Out of ninety-five applications of Article XIX from 1950 to 1978, it was applied only twice by LDCs—Nigeria in 1961 and Peru in 1963 (L/4679).[3]

The Article does not stipulate which types of protective measures can be resorted to (i.e. tariff increases or introduction of quotas). It specifically mentions the withdrawal of tariff concessions (that is, the increase of a bound duty rate) but there is no reference to quantitative restrictions. From the *travaux préparatoires* for GATT it appears that quantitative restrictions are also permitted, and in practice they have indeed been employed. Several restrictions are attached to the invocation of this safeguard. Firstly, any action under Article XIX is subject to the rule of non-discrimination among suppliers. Emergency actions should be taken in respect of the product in question and not in respect of the particular countries. There is only one case in which Article XIX action has been taken on a discriminatory basis unequivocally aimed at a single source of supply. This was the British action to restrict imports of television sets from South Korea in 1975 (L/4679).[4]

Secondly, the protective measures, tariff increases or quantitative restrictions, are only intended as temporary palliatives given that the object is only to delay and not to nullify the immediate impact of foreign competition on the old-established producers. During the life of these temporary restrictions these affected producers are given time to adjust to the pressure of imports.

In the third place, the affected exporter countries have the right to demand a compensatory concession to preserve the balance of their trading advantages. Alternatively, should there be no agreement on compensation, the exporting government can retaliate by withdrawing an equivalent concession.

The MFA which provides a stamp of legitimacy for the selective protection of textile and clothing industries of the developed countries involves an explicit waiver by all parties of their rights and obligations under Article XIX. On the one hand, importing countries are free from their MFN obligation: they can determine which suppliers are the ones disrupting their markets and request them and only them to control the flow of their exports. A central feature of both the LTA and the MFA is that they have circumscribed the controls to imports from LDCs (initially, Japan was also included). The

United States and the West European countries exempted their own products from the quota restrictions on the grounds that these did not create 'market disruption'.[5] On the other hand, exporting countries have waived their right to retaliate by withdrawing a concession as well as their right to demand an equivalent concession in compensation for the restrictions on textiles and clothing.

4.5 MARKET DISRUPTION AND ORDERLY MARKETING

Central to the textile trade restrictions is the concept of market disruption. It provided the rationale for the MFA and its precursors the Short-Term Arrangement and the Long-Term Arrangement on Cotton Textiles.

The description of market disruption (see transcription in Section 4.2) had from the very start elements of discrimination. Not only are 'particular sources' mentioned but there is also an emphasis on the lower price at which these sources are able to sell the products. These prices are genuinely low; despite not being the result of dumping, a penalty is justified. The target of discrimination was further circumscribed by clarifying that the reference to 'governmental intervention' did not include the pricing practices of centrally planned economies (BISD, 9th S, 1961, p. 108).

GATT had been intended to provide the framework for the smooth expansion of international trade on the basis of comparative advantage and international specialization. Yet the description of a disrupted market rested precisely on the refusal to admit lower costs as a reason for the growth of trade. It is ironic that a committee should be set up in GATT to study 'the relevance to international trade and differences in the cost of various factors of production and marketing, including labour costs' (BISD, 9th S, 1961, p. 28). In other words, to analyse the relevance of comparative advantages to international trade, this being supposedly the theoretical underpinning of GATT.

The notion of market disruption and labour costs became intimately connected; that the marriage should take place in the textile and clothing sector is due to its being a preeminently labour-intensive sector and a price competitive market: 'businesses where cost is the sole basis for competitive advantage' (Courtalds, *Annual Report*, 1980–1, p. 10). As we have seen in the preceding chapter, price competition in world trade has largely declined relative to product differentiation.

Initially, the situation of market disruption was seen as a problem of the speed at which trade had grown. Writers generally devoted to the free-trade philosophy saw the derogation of GATT's rules as a positive sign. 'This is almost an economist's dream', wrote Curzon (1965, p. 257). What was thought praiseworthy about the situation was that the protection-inclined governments were seen to be asking only for temporary measures to smoothen the abrupt disappearance of their old-established industries; they were seen to be implicitly accepting, therefore, that factors of production would ultimately have to be withdrawn from the industries which had lost their comparative advantage. GATT would be supervising the reallocation of resources—a process which would contribute to raising global efficiency and welfare. Yet the concept of market disruption also implicitly implied that the exporting country took responsibility for controlling the flow of its exports so as not to flood the market of the importing country. By admitting responsibility the exporter surrendered its rights to demand compensation or impose retaliation. As noted by Sidney Golt, at the time of the drafting of the Havana Charter, the view was that trade was disrupted by the measures introduced to restrict imports, whereas the climate of opinion has shifted to seeing exports as the disturbing element in a given order (Golt, 1978, p. 13).

In theory, GATT was envisaged as codifying a system in which market access would be a right to be earned through price competition and efficiency. In practice, GATT supervised a system in which price competition had faded into the background and the factors we have traced in Chapter 3 took over. When competitive newcomers arrived on the scene GATT could not but preserve the existing balance, rather than steer the old-established producers out.

The problem of changing market shares and the limited role GATT could play to accommodate newcomers surfaced in many forms. Simultaneous with the textile issue, a dispute arose over butter exports to the British market. The conflict in this case was not a conflict between domestic and foreign producers but one between old-established and new exporters. In March 1961 the Government of New Zealand requested multilateral consultation on the marketing of butter in Britain, its traditional market, since its market share had declined from 40 per cent in 1958 to 36 per cent in 1960. The problem was seen as one in which 'small suppliers had delivered more significant quantities and have taken a great share of the market' (GATT, BISD, 10th S., 1961, p. 75). The working group formed for the purpose of studying the problem recommended 'more orderly marketing arrangements'. The Executive Secretary of GATT thereupon held individual consultations with the delegations of the exporting countries to 'ascertain whether general agreement could be reached on figures for country-by-country shipments' (L/1720, p. 10). These consultations revealed no possibility of reaching agreement and Britain ended by taking unilateral action in the form of a system of import quotas based on historical shares to be enforced from 1962 (GATT, BISD, 10th S, 1961, pp. 74, 77). At the Ministerial Meeting of November 1961 the New Zealand Trade Minister expressed his satisfaction with the course taken.

Although butter is an agricultural product and the present study is not generally concerned with this area of international trade, two points can be drawn from the case which are of relevance to the course of the textile controversy. In the first place, the initial steps in the consultation aimed at achieving a compromise among the exporters for mutual respect of traditional market shares. When the exporters failed to agree on quotas for 'orderly marketing', the initiative was removed from their hands and unilateral quotas imposed by Britain. In the second place, the resolution of the conflict tended to create 'orderly marketing' by taking into consideration past performance of exporters; it favoured the firstcomer by recognizing its right to retain a market share. This course of action was probably more regardful of New Zealand's interests than a compromise solution would have been. British unilateral quotas could more easily be unmindful of the right of newcomers to increase their market access. In the resolution of conflicts, respect for the *status quo* tends to prevail. 'The club's fundamental view is that the balance of trading advantages between any one nation and the rest of the world shall not be upset' (Shonfield, 1976, p. 127).

4.6 AMERICAN LEADERSHIP

From 1945 until the 1960s, the United States and Great Britain were the major producers and exporters of cotton textiles, being at the same time significant importers, thanks to relatively liberal import policies compared with the rest of the developed countries.[6] Textile manufacturers in these countries were thus the first to feel the competition from lower-cost countries and to demand special treatment for textile imports. The nature of the problem was, however, different in each country. Traditionally, the Lancashire industry had been reliant on world markets and import policies were relatively liberal. Alongside decolonization came the thrust towards import substitution and the consequent erosion of British export markets. Between 1913 and 1955 Britain's textile exports fell by 75 per cent in real terms (Keesing & Wolf, 1980, p. 9). The United States, on the other hand, had a longer and consistent history of protectionism in textiles. Initially, however, American regulations did not have a discriminatory profile: Japanese goods until 1957 were not subject to any specific controls, only to the same tariff as all other sources. With import policies that were a residue of its imperial interests, the British home market was losing ground to a different source. On the one hand, Commonwealth goods were allowed access totally free from both tariffs and quotas; on the other, on the accession of Japan to GATT in 1955, Britain (as well as fourteen other countries) immediately sought a shield and proceeded to invoke Article XXXV which excused it from applying GATT rules to Japan for as long as it wished.[7]

Both in the United States and Britain, policy came to be significantly shaped by pressure from the domestic industries, but it was the United States that took the initiative in justifying protection under GATT, both in the early

1960s when the cotton industry was in trouble, in the 1970s when the problem had extended to man-made fibres and in the 1980s when other natural fibres were brought under the MFA umbrella. The first voluntary export quotas were implemented by Japan in response to requests from the United States in December 1955. By January 1957 Japan had delineated a five-year plan of export restrictions to satisfy American pressure.

In Britain, government involvement first took a different route. The Cotton Industry Act of 1959 introduced a programme of adjustment assistance to the industry which comprised: a system of cash payments to firms scrapping plant with a premium for those leaving the industry altogether; financial subsidies to firms undertaking approved schemes of re-equipment; and compensation to workers who were left jobless as a result of the subsidized modernization. The industry also lobbied for a formal quota on cotton imports from the Asian Commonwealth countries which had hitherto been free of either duties or quotas. Failure on this front led the industry to look for short-term expedients in a privately negotiated export restraint for 1959–61 with the three major Commonwealth suppliers, Hong Kong, India and Pakistan. The Lancashire Pact, as it came to be known, proved not to be totally effective for the industry's purpose. Imports from other sources continued to grow until, in 1966, the Government itself imposed a quota on all imports of cotton textiles covering yarns and fabrics and made-up goods containing over 50 per cent of cotton by weight for five years, ending in 1970. Commonwealth imports were still allowed to come in duty-free. When the quota controls were due to expire, the industry recommended the shift from *ad hoc* quantity restrictions to tariff protection. In 1972 a tariff was finally imposed on Commonwealth goods that brought them into line with the MFN tariff, while quota controls remained in force on all cotton textile imports. Quotas were extended in the mid-1970s to cover wool and man-made fibres taking advantage of the expansion of the LTA into the MFA in 1974.

American initiatives requesting export restraint from Japan have been traced in Gerard and Victoria Curzon's study of trade relations under the GATT (Curzon and Curzon, 1976, p. 263 ff.). The United States was the sole country not practising discrimination against competitive Japanese imports. By 1956 imports of cotton textiles had grown to 1937 levels, representing 1.7 per cent of domestic production, but Japanese cotton textiles accounted for over 60 per cent of total imports. Such successful expansion was bound to put the industry onto the defensive. To compound the problem, a price support system for cotton growers was instated in 1955 (and this remained in force for ten years) and so the price of the industry's raw material rose relative to the world market. Faced with this situation, the industry approached the US Tariff Commission with four petitions to apply Article XIX of GATT (US, International Trade Commission, 1978, p. 1). The petitions were rejected; the Administration was not willing to pay the costs that Article XIX involved.

Invocation of Article XIX meant tariff renegotiation with other GATT members without in any case offering domestic industry a greater sense of security since Article XIX does not permit selective treatment against a specific source. Furthermore, the United States had been pushing the Europeans to admit Japan to GATT from 1952 to 1955, and could hardly, as soon as it had been successful, apply an escape clause against its godchild. Yet another powerful consideration stopped the Eisenhower Administration from going to GATT:

> it had recently over-played the GATT's waiver provisions by asking for (and obtaining) a broadly-termed waiver to restrict agricultural products from entering the United States, without the customary time limits. It is no exaggeration to say that this incident had caused GATT's first major crisis and had resulted in a considerable loss of confidence in the United States as the leader and principle proponent of freer world trade. . . . It was therefore politically the worst possible moment for the United States to address itself once more to GATT (in the name of self-seeking protectionism) and ask permission from the Europeans (essentially) to restrict its imports from Japan. [Curzon & Curzon, 1976, p. 258.]

Yet the Administration was not unsympathetic to the claims of industry, even though, as mentioned above, total imports constituted less than 2 per cent of domestic production. The conflict between 'self-seeking protectionism' and free trade for other markets was resolved with Japanese goodwill. The petitions for Article XIX safeguards, though unsuccessful, had brought the problem home and had given the Administration a justification and a bargaining counter for approaching the Japanese with a five-year programme of voluntary export quotas. The compromise reached with Japan to satisfy the textile industry rendered possible a round of trade liberalization. Congress extended the Reciprocal Trade Agreement Act and hence gave President Eisenhower authority for initiating the Dillon Round of Trade negotiations (Bergsten, 1975, p. 253).

The conflict in American trade interests was not, however, a new phenomenon. Suffice it to recall that the ITO floundered on Congressional approval, though the proposal had been conceived by Department of State officials with a wider vision of American influence. When drafting the General Agreement, the United States had also introduced a double standard: while quantitative restrictions for industrial protection were forbidden (Article XI), they were permitted for the agricultural sector at the request of the Department of Agriculture in order to allow the United States to continue its price support programme. In 1960 Eric Wyndham White, then Executive Secretary of GATT, conceded that Article XI had been 'largely tailor-made to US requirements' (quoted in Dam, 1970, p. 260). The textile sector was to demonstrate that this clearcut separation between agriculture and industry could not always be fully sustained.

The Japanese expedient was ephemeral. Although Japan was effectively restrained, her share of cotton textile imports to the United States, declining from 63 per cent in 1958 to 26 per cent in 1960, the slack was swiftly taken up by Hong Kong (through trans-shipment or directly from Hong Kong-based manufacturers), whose share of cotton textile imports rose from 14 to 27.5 per cent (US, International Trade Commission, 1978, p. 3). The value of these exports leapt from $3.6 million in 1956, when Japan first began to regulate her exports, to $108 million in 1958, thus exposing a potential threat. The government of Hong Kong was approached with a quota scheme but turned it down. Furthermore, Portugal, Egypt, Taiwan, Spain, Pakistan and India had also come into the world textile market—somewhat aided by the United States farm programme which had raised above those prices prevailing in the world market the price of cotton to domestic mills.

Kennedy's electoral campaign in 1959 promised the industry more effective rescue; Kennedy redeemed the pledge on 2 May 1961, issuing a textile programme which among other measures requested the Department of State to 'seek an international understanding which will provide a basis for trade that will avoid undue disruption of established industries' (US, International Trade Commission, 1978, p. 7). The result was the interim Short-Term Arrangement extended into the Long-Term Arrangement for a five-year period from 1962 to 1967. In essence, the STA and the LTA legalized the restrictions on Japan and authorized negotiations with reluctant suppliers (Curzon & Curzon, 1976, p. 178; Dam, 1970, p. 300; Keesing & Wolf, 1980, p. 16).[8]

The LTA 'promised enough protection to cause a group of 75 interested Congressmen to thank President Kennedy' (*New York Times*, 16 February 1962, quoted in Curzon & Curzon, 1976, p. 178). Once again, the appeasement of the textile industry served to pave the way for Congressional approval of the Trade Expansion Act of 1962 which conferred on the President the authority to initiate the Kennedy Round of GATT trade negotiations.

This tug of war between the two industrial sectors of the American economy, the one whose production was largely internationalized serving to spur the movement towards world trade liberalization versus another, more inward-orientated trying to stall the effects of foreign trade in the home market, was re-staged under Nixon, and yet another compromise had to be reached. Again, Nixon's Presidential campaign of 1968 pledged further import relief to the textile industry which by now claimed protection over the whole range of textile products through all stages of production, from yarns to clothing and all types of fibre, both natural (cotton and wool) and artificial. This time, however, Japanese goodwill was less forthcoming and at one point Senate ratification for the return of the Okinawa base to Japanese jurisdiction seemed to be conditional on the conclusion of a textile agreement (Curzon & Curzon, 1976, p. 268; Destler, 1979, p. 315; Cooper, 1973, p. 257). Impasse on the textile front lasted until Nixon's new economic policy in 1971 (with devaluation of the dollar and a 10 per cent surcharge on imports). In October the Japanese conceded and signed a three-year agreement (1971–4) covering their exports of wool, artificial and cotton products—'a forced settlement sqeeezed out of the Japanese government at its time of maximum vulnerability'. (Destler, 1978, p. 315). Further agreements were subsequently reached with Hong Kong, South Korea and Taiwan. President Nixon's desire to secure reelection contributed to the timing.

The issue was then ushered into GATT, which carried out an extensive review of all textile trade (L/3797, 1972). In the course of 1973, when the LTA was to expire, negotiations for extending coverage to wool and man-made fibres were initiated, and resulted in the MFA, which entered into force on 1 January 1974. The initiative removed an important obstacle to Congressional approval of the 1974 Trade Act, the statute which was to authorize executive participation in the Tokyo Round of multilateral trade negotiations (Keesing & Wolf, 1980, p. 17; Bergsten, 1975, p. 253).

The successful conclusion of the Tokyo Round negotiations in 1979 depended once again on reaching a bargain to placate the textile companies and unions. In autumn 1978, nearing the final stages of the Tokyo Round, Congress attempted to pass a bill barring President Carter from offering tariff cuts on textiles. The bill was initially vetoed by Carter but in November he reversed his stance and made a statement indicating that assistance to the industry would be forthcoming (*The Financial Times*, 12 November 1978). Shortly afterwards Carter issued a policy paper with a textile programme which announced that

> the administration is determined to assist the beleaguered [sic] textile and apparel industry and is committed to its health and growth [because] this industry provides employment for almost two and a half million people, the largest single source of jobs in our manufacturing economy, and provides our consumers with a reliable, competitively priced, vital source for all the many vital clothing, medical, military, industrial and other products of this modern technology [US Department of Commerce, International Trade Administration, News Release, 15 February 1979, p. 1.]

The programme was described as 'an integral part' of the Tokyo Round and pledged that import surges under the MFA would be 'aggressively controlled' (p. 2). It also promised 'full and prior industry and labour consultation on strategy, outlook and problems with respect to bilateral agreements'. It provided a snap-back clause so that the MFN tariffs on products negotiated during the Tokyo Round would revert to previous levels should the MFA not be renewed when due in 1982. Should renewal fail, the

President agreed to request a mandate from Congress to impose unilateral control on imports. Moreover, textiles would be excluded from the government procurement code which was part of the trade-freeing drive of the Tokyo Round on non-tariff barriers. As a quid pro quo, industry agreed 'to make maximum effort to maintain international competitiveness, to the promoting of efficiency within the industry, to continue to act responsibly pursuant to the President's anti-inflation program guidelines, and to support the national trade policies' (p. 8). The programme then gave Carter a free hand to offer a MFN tariff cut on textiles (i.e. fabrics) of 30 per cent and on knitted sweaters from 42 to 17 per cent in exchange for an EEC cut on textiles of 27 per cent (*The Financial Times*, 5 April 1979). Subsequent to this deal, the existing MFA bilateral agreements with Hong Kong, South Korea and Taiwan were reopened to introduce tighter controls for their remaining life and a new agreement was drawn up with China (US International Trade Commission, 1983, p. 3 and *The Financial Times*, 20 August 1979).

Finally, Reagan's Administration had its own turn, at the time of the renegotiation of the MFA in 1981. The initial American stance seemed committed to greater liberalization yet, as the last week approached, the American delegation suddenly reversed its position and issued a statement announcing that 'a recent worsening of the textile economy in the US has forced Washington to take a tougher stance' (*The Financial Times*, 12 December 1981). It was also the responsibility of the Reagan Administration to extend the coverage of the MFA to natural fibres other than wool and cotton when the 1986 renegotiation took place prior to the launching of the Punta del Este Round.

It is reasonable to conclude, as Burford Brandeis does, that 'the need for handling textile imports matters parallel and separate from general trade negotiations is well-established as a key facet of US trade policy' (in Keesing & Wolf, 1980, p. 43). The history also shows a policy of having to make one step backward to placate the textile industry for every step forward required by sectors interested in foreign markets. The dualism of American trade interests was reproduced in GATT as a natural development of American economic prominence. As in other respects, the GATT could not but be 'the international counterpart of US tariff policy' (Meyer, 1978, p. 126). Kindleberger (1978) has argued that an hegemonic leader is a requisite for a liberal world economic order. The United States as an hegemonic leader also played a crucial role in initiating and legitimizing protectionist policies under the GATT.

Yet the American initiative to place the quota system under GATT's aegis and thus achieve legitimacy for existing quotas as well as obtain a free hand to keep potential threats at bay could not have succeeded as easily without crucial European support. This support also came naturally. The pressures from lower-wage countries already being felt in Europe were strengthened by fears of diversion of imports into European markets as a consequence of American restrictions. In the Kennedy Round the EEC insisted on an extension of the LTA as a condition to its MFN tariff reduction. For the renegotiation of the MFA in 1978 the EEC introduced the 'reasonable departures' clause and the Nordic countries claimed that they needed special prerogatives to protect their 'minimum viable production'.[9] Followers can and do add an impetus of their own to the trend set in motion by the United States.

4.7 MARKET STRUCTURE OF THE TEXTILE SECTOR

At the heart of the matter are the particular features of the textile sector. Neoclassical economics, of which the GATT was an institutional offspring, regards the textile regulations as a major departure from the post-war principles of free trade conducted according to comparative advantage. GATT was to be an international institution dedicated to ensuring that market access would be a right to be obtained through price competition. In the words of the GATT staff, the MFA was 'the first important instance in which the generally and solemnly agreed rules of post-war policy conduct— including the keystone of the system, the non-discrimination role—were formally set aside for reasons recognized as pragmatic' (Blackhurst *et al.*, 1977, p. 48). This departure is one of the 'stepping-stones to the present crisis in international commercial policy' (Blackhurst *et al.*, 1977, p. 48). The MFA is viewed as the result of two factors: 'refusal to adjust' to a compelling change in the international pattern of comparative advantages and the unchecked power of vested interests organized as protectionist lobbies. In contrast, free trade is endowed with political virtues. 'In every country it is supported by a loose coalition, which has to be assiduously cultivated and which could not be held together without moves ensuring visible, publicly defensible fairness in competition with foreign firms' (Tumlir, 1979, p. 253). The Curzons argue similarly that 'While the forces for protection are concentrated and politically active, the forces for free trade are diffused and politically silent' (Curzon & Curzon, 1976, p. 157). A further step towards economic reductionism in the same direction is the implication that whereas protectionism is backed by vested interests, free trade goes hand in hand with 'the decentralised political order that guarantees individual freedom' (Blackhurst *et al.*, 1977, p. 57) because 'every policy interference with the economic process which limits its efficiency creates a vested interest, and the precedent inviting other interests to organise and assert collective power' (p. 51).

The underlying assumption is that all sectors share similar operational features. International trade is then seen as an incrementalist process in which failure to sustain the momentum towards liberalization precipitates retreat into mutually destructive protectionism—a paradigm that Susan Strange has called the 'Alcoholic's Anonymous' view of international trade. The essence of the argument is that at the domestic level 'capitulation' to protectionist pressures in one industrial sector compels to capitulation in other sectors. 'Relapse into trade wars, as into hopeless alcoholic dependence, would soon follow' (Strange, 1979, p. 330). The brief history outlined above indicates that in practice there is no logically necessary correlation between protectionism in one sector and protectionism in another, rather a dual policy can be hammered out feeding upon and fuelling movement in opposite directions for different sectors with different outlooks, one that derives profits from international business, the other that operates profitably on the basis of the domestic market and is placated before every liberalizing drive.

In the preceding chapter I have argued that intra-industrial specialization was central to post-war trade liberalization. With intra-industry trade, countries found benefits in the reduction of tariffs on products they both imported and exported. Industrial development depended on imports as much as on exports. The lobby supporting and spurring free trade can thus no longer be seen as a 'loose coalition'. With industrial sectors becoming largely research and development intensive, markets became increasingly less open to new entrants and price competition among firms declined relative to competition on the basis of product differentiation. In contrast, the textile sector remained mostly an open, price-competitive market. It produces largely standard bulk production and market niches cannot be carved as easily in the way of differentiated products. These special features make it an accessible sector for LDCs, on the one hand, and on the other, a particularly unruly sector.

4.7.1 Subsectors

The textile sector comprises all activities by which fibres are transformed through processing. It is a vast sector covering several processes and fibres. The LTA covered only cotton yarns, fabrics and goods; the MFA extended its coverage into wool, man-made fibres and blends. In a general sense the term textiles refers to the production of fibres, yarns and fabrics as well as to the made-up goods (garments, household furnishing, etc.). A narrower definition distinguishes between the production of yarns and fabrics on the one hand, and the finished article on the other.

For the purposes of our analysis here, a division will be made between three closely linked subsectors of the complex textiles family: (a) the cotton industry, which includes spinning of yarns, threads and fabric manufacturing through knitting and weaving; (b) the man-made fibre industry; (c) clothing production using cotton and other natural fibres as well as man-made fibres.

In cotton-growing economies, the cotton industry is a direct outgrowth of its primary producing sector. This is the case with a great number of LDCs (as well as the United States, the Soviet Union and China) which embarked on spinning and weaving as a natural extension of their cotton-growing activities. Cotton is produced in over eighty countries so that world production is dispersed despite American leadership in both production and trade. For many of these countries, who are relatively small producers by world standards, cotton is a crucial foreign-exchange earner (e.g. Nicaragua, Mali, Egypt, Sudan); they have an obvious interest in carrying out domestically as many stages of processing as possible so that value added is increased and their foreign exchange earnings are boosted. Many of these countries therefore offer their national industries cotton at prices well below world market level or levy export taxes on raw cotton or offer other subsidies or tax incentives to encourage industrialization. Another perceived benefit of processing lies in greater price stability as compared to the unprocessed commodity. Furthermore, the raw cotton trade is dominated by the giant commodity trading corporations, such as Cargill, Ralli Brothers, etc. (UNCTAD, *Fibres and Textiles* . . .); so processing offered LDCs what seemed to be the added advantage of greater national control over their export trade. To the extent that this has been achieved, it led to another cul-de-sac, as is evidenced by the Agreements that we are examining.

This 'global mushrooming' of the cotton industry is facilitated by its labour-intensive character which makes it not only attractive in terms of employment creation but also (and more important for the purposes of this discussion), being technically straightforward, a relatively easy industry to enter. Technical knowledge is diffused and there are no patent restrictions that can regulate output and trade. Cotton processing is thus by nature a fiercely competitive industry. Competition keeps profit rates down and leads to a high turnover of firms.

The man-made fibre industry is by nature an oligopolized sector. Its main feature is difficulty of entry. Man-made fibre companies tend to have close corporate links with the chemical and petrochemical industries and are an essential outlet for their production. In Western Europe, for example, the chemical fibres sector absorbs 25 per cent of the total production of the petrochemical industry (*European Report*, 1977, p. 2). Concentration in these sectors is inevitable because of the high capital costs, as well as the long lead times before investment results are profitable. Man-made fibres have been developed by the chemical corporations, devoting substantial sums to research and development over long periods. For example, the Dupont Corporation devoted more than ten years and an expenditure of about $30 million to put nylon hosiery on sale in the United States in 1940 (UNCTAD, *International Trade* . . ., p. 37). Such firms hold patent rights over their products, so that concentration persists irrespective of whether they engage directly in production or not. It has been estimated that Rhône-Poulenc, for example, produces as much as 85 per cent of all French man-made fibres; in

Italy Montedison (and associated Snia Viscosa) also accounted for 85 per cent of Italian chemical fibres (UNCTAD, *Fibres and Textiles* . . ., 1980, pp. 146–7). Entry in this sector is difficult because it is capital- and research-intensive; this has meant that LDCs do not have indigenous or autonomous production capacity as they do with cotton. Those LDCs that have ventured into the man-made fibre industry have had to rely on foreign investment or foreign licences. Another distinguishing feature of this sector which can be inferred from the above figures and examples is the predominantly national orientation of production. The home base of these corporations is still where most of investment and sales are concentrated. For example, in 1980 the home base provided Dupont with 68 per cent of its sales (either as home sales or exports) and 80 per cent of its investments are concentrated there (*Annual Report*, 1980). Seventy per cent of Courtaulds' sales in 1981 were carried out in or from Britain; 65 per cent of its investment is located in this market (*Annual Report*, 1981). Similar trends can be detected for the other man-made fibre corporations.

The Paris-based industry organization Comité Internationale de la Rayonne et des Fibres Synthétiques (CIRFS) argued in a study carried out in 1976, *The Future of the Man-Made Fibre Industry in Western Europe*, that transport costs make it difficult for European producers to make a profit on delivery to distant markets, 'so only local markets can ensure a future for Europe's man-made fibre industry . . . particularly in the light of the world-wide development of man-made fibre capacity to satisfy local industry's demand for fibres' (pp. 32–3). Furthermore, since more than 50 per cent of their output goes to the European clothing industry, the erosion of this industry concerned the man-made fibre producers and the chemical and the petrochemical corporations as well. 'The loss of the local market would make it difficult to achieve economies of scale which are essential in the modern technological branches'. The attendant increasing cost, it argued, would endanger export competitiveness.

The evidence thus indicates a predominantly national character of operations in this sector, a trend that has a spill-over effect into the (by nature) less oligopolized clothing industry in developed countries, because of its importance as an end-user of textiles.

The clothing industry is a major end-user of textiles. In Western Europe, for example, 55 per cent of fibres are used for apparel, 30 per cent for household furnishings and 15 per cent for industrial ends (UNCTAD, *Fibres and Textiles* . . ., p. 201). Because of this pivotal role it was natural that it should become closely associated, even absorbed in some cases, by the chemical fibre producers. Most chemical and fibre corporations have actively pursued a policy of securing captive outlets by bolstering their vulnerable customers in a variety of ways (buying companies, lending money for re-equipment and seeking to shield them from imports). The result has been the

close integration of the petrochemical, chemical, textile and clothing industries, and the increasing sophistication of production and marketing techniques in developed countries. The lead was taken in the United Kingdom by
ICI and Courtaulds which, since the early 1960s, simultaneously with the
enforcement of the LTA moved downstream to secure businesses which used
or could potentially use their fibre output, the result of which was a process of
increased capital concentration in the industry. The LTA should be seen in
this light essentially as a pre-emptive exercise destined to ease the substitution
of cotton by man-made fibres and the transformation of the industry. The
shield from highly competitive imports provided by the LTA allowed a rise in
investment by arresting the decline in profits. 'Protection does not create the
motive, but it greatly facilitates the means by raising profitability, which
increases the willingness to invest, the internal generation of funds and the
ability to borrow' (Keesing & Wolf, 1980, p. 120).

Despite this suction movement, the clothing industry overall remains a
technically straightforward business characterized by ease of entry and
labour-intensive production. To be sure, there are a few major firms selling
differentiated products in the way of branded goods. Nevertheless, apparel
production is overwhelmingly carried out by fairly competitive small-scale
businesses with limited managerial and financial resources—a feature shared
both by developed and less-developed countries. Sweatshops, though more
conspicuous in LDCs, can still be seen in developed countries where they
tend to employ immigrant and female labour. In the United States, as
mentioned earlier, two-thirds of all firms have less than fifty employees (*South*
August 1983, p. 61). Levi Strauss and Blue Bell, two of the biggest clothing
firms hold only a small fraction of the market. Competition is fierce, even at
the national level, and profits are thereby pushed downwards. For most of
these firms, the additional competition from LDCs, with their dispro-
portionately lower labour costs (Figure 3.1) will inevitably mean bankruptcy.

'Apparel manufacture is the most labour-intensive of all industries.'
(Morawetz, 1982, p. 92). Labour costs rather than any other raw material
input remain a major element in determining prices. The significance of this
can best be grasped by the fact that 'the quintupling of oil in the mid-seventies
had practically no effect on the price of synthetic finished products' (CIRFS,
1976, p. 34). Thus, although for cotton-growing LDCs there may be a
difference between exports of cotton products and man-made fibre clothing
which lies in the processing of an indigenous raw material, labour-rich LDCs
can still enjoy a significant comparative advantage in the production of
clothing. These countries are the success stories of South-east Asia, South
Korea, Taiwan and Hong Kong especially. Not being 'tied' to cotton
production, they are able to follow with ease the structural change that
occurred in the industry in the 1970s as a result of the relative decline of cotton
and the widespread and accelerated popularization of synthetics and their

blends. Similarly in the 1980s they were easily able to switch to natural fibres other than those restrained by the MFA. As all fibres were imported, replacement involved painless adjustments. Moreover, the controls on cotton goods imposed by the LTA in the early 1960s and on wool and man-made fibres in the 1970s provided ready-made incentives for the switch into the as yet unrestricted fibres. Subsequently, South Korea and and Taiwan in particular, actively pursued foreign assistance to develop production and exports which led to close links with the Japanese companies. These non-cotton producing LDCs succeeded in building up the manufacture of clothing for exports and obtaining a sizeable share of the world market. LDCs' share of world trade in apparel grew from 19 to 25 per cent between 1965 and 1973; by 1983 the share had grown to 42 per cent despite stricter MFA measures.

4.7.2 International investment

While trade in textiles, and especially clothing, accelerated, the international-ization of capital in the sector lagged behind. Multinational corporations (MNCs) tend to play a relatively small role in the international trade of apparel and intra-firm trade is much less frequent than in other export sectors of LDCs. Trade as well as production is overwhelmingly carried out by national companies exporting native products in large quantities, and threatens to dislocate established producers in developed countries. These are precisely the comparative advantages of traditional explanations of inter-national trade. The marginal role of MNCs in this trade sector can be grasped by comparing the figures in Table 4.1 below, which accounts for imports into the United States that are carried out between related firms. These are here defined to include buyer firms related through ownership to the exporter by 5 per cent or more equity stock. Even such a broad definition of intra-firm trade shows that in this sector independent imports consist of a larger share than for other manufactured goods (except footwear).[10] At any rate, clothing is the only large category of imports that originates predominantly both in LDCs and in independent firms. By contrast, in electrical machinery, which has also experienced buoyant export growth, production is internationalized under subcontracting and intra-firm arrangements. Export growth, rather than dislocating established producers, is closely linked to their investment patterns and wider interests so that the comparative advantage that LDCs may hold are internalized by firms in developed countries. In this sense the electrical and electronic goods industry is the antipode of fabrics and apparel. The comparative advantages enjoyed by LDCs from lower labour costs are held by unrelated firms and lead to extreme polarization threatening to dislocate established producers in developed countries—'market disruption' in GATT's terminology.

Table 4.1 United States related-party imports as a percentage of total imports by category

	Percentage			Import value ($m)	
	OECD	LDCs	Total	Total	LDCs
1. textile yarn, fabrics & made-up articles	35.1	7.8	22.6	1,776	736
2. machinery other than electric	60.3	63.5	60.3	9,777	658
3. electrical machinery, apparatus & appliances	55.2	75.2	63.4	8,451	3,541
4. transport equipment	84.7	32.6	83.9	18,229	304
5. clothing	12.0	11.5	11.3	4,049	3,221
6. footwear	11.7	4.4	7.3	1,890	1,031
7. professional & scientific instruments	50.9	51.2	50.9	2,316	488

Source: Helleiner (1981) from US Bureau of Census, Foreign Trade Division (IQ 246).

This does not imply that there is a total absence of foreign investment in the textile sector of LDCs, but such investment as there is has hitherto been only marginally 'trade orientated' (Kojima, 1975). Most foreign direct investment is concentrated in the upstream chemical, petrochemical and synthetic fibres complex—a capital- and research-intensive sector. This is only *partly* because foreign direct investment was defensive or tariff-jumping in its purpose. If this were the sole reason MNCs might have invested in clothing for the same tariff-jumping motive. The main reason lies in the origins of foreign direct investment in manufacturing in LDCs. As innumerable studies have shown, MNCs in these countries tend to be concentrated in industries in which barriers of entry to new producers are among the highest, in industries with oligopolistic characteristics (economies of scale, high capital intensity, advanced technology, heavy financial outlays, and so forth) (Hymer, 1976; Dunning, 1970; Vernon, 1971). In contrast to the production of natural fibres and clothing, these are the sectors which LDCs could not enter on their own account. This setting-up of foreign subsidiaries aimed to serve local markets and consequently involved duplication of the business developed in the home base or other production sites. For example, while a third of ICI's assets are located abroad, a spokesman for the company noted that 'the existence of these plants does not reduce export sales (from the United Kingdom), for they have the effect of priming the export pump and give rise to additional opportunities for exports from the United Kingdom' (UNCTAD, *Fibres and Textiles* ..., 1980, p. 145). In short, foreign subsidiaries are export destinations rather than production sites for the home market of the parent company.

There are two exceptions to this general picture, both of which are factors operating in the evolution of the MFA. The first concerns Japanese investment which has unique characteristics. The other is an incipient trend among some firms in Europe and in the United States towards international specialization.

4.7.3 Japanese foreign direct investment

A particular feature of Japanese investment abroad, as was noted previously, is that it has mostly been channelled to LDCs, in contrast to European and American companies that have invested predominantly in each other's market. Sixty per cent of total Japanese investment abroad goes to LDCs and mostly to its neighbours in South Asia, Hong Kong, South Korea, Taiwan, Thailand, Singapore, etc. (World Bank, 1979, pp. 4–5). This same trend is evident in the textile industry to the extent that a considerable share of the export growth of many of these South Asian countries can be attributed to Japanese extension overseas. In South Korea the leading textile company, Sam Sung, has a joint venture in synthetics with the Japanese trading conglomerate Mitsui and also with its textile subsidiary, Toray. Toray is also the major shareholder of the leading Hong Kong company, The Textile Alliance Group (UNCTAD, *Fibres and Textiles* . . .; 1980, pp. 187–8).

A decisive generator of the expansion of Japanese textile business abroad was undoubtedly the imposition of restraints on its own exports. Yet evasion of import quotas has not been the only motive. Apparently, it is also Japanese policy to export its lowest-wage, lowest-productivity industries—such as textiles—and so to maintain the dynamism of its domestic industrial base. According to Kojima (1975), foreign investment in manufacturing had until then been mainly confined to such traditional industries as textiles, clothing and the processing of steel, in which Japan has been losing its comparative advantage. Ozawa's extensive study of Japanese foreign investment notes that the substantial rise in the value of the yen has been the major cause spurring production abroad. Revaluation

> decisively eroded the price competitiveness of most of Japan's labour intensive traditional exports, such as textiles and electrical appliances. In order to retain trade competitiveness, Japanese firms, especially the smaller ones, were compelled to transplant production to other Asian countries where labour costs continued to be lower than at home. The increased buying power of the yen relative to the dollar also gave them a financial incentive, as Japanese firms were able to acquire foreign assets at much lower costs in those Asian countries whose currencies were closely tied to the dollar [Ozawa, 1979, p. 96.]

As a result a closer, and ever deepening economic interdependence has developed between Japan and each of those Asian countries that adopted an outward-looking strategy for economic development. Thereby, while the number of South Asian countries that are requested to limit their exports to Europe and the United States grows, quotas on Japanese exports have become obsolescent. Although Japan produces one-sixth of the world's synthetic fibres and is the second world producer after the United States (UNCTAD, *Fibres and Textiles* . . ., 1980, p. 148), the EEC does not have a bilateral textile agreement with Japan. The Japanese quotas for the American market tend to remain largely unfulfilled. In effect, since 1978, the Agreement between Japan and the United States has been amended to have merely a consultative function: limitations are not actually enforced but negotiations may be proposed should imports reach a certain specified level (US, International Trade Commission, 1978, p. 48).

The particular pattern of Japanese foreign investment (allowing intra-industry and intra-firm trade with South Asian countries) also means that Japan itself does not have to employ quotas to restrict its imports, despite having a growing deficit in clothing trade totally accounted for by LDC sources (Keesing & Wolf, 1980, p. 81). Although import policies are not free of regulation, Japan has not resorted to the international framework provided by GATT and the MFA.

The close connection between Japan and the dynamic exporters of South Asia is not only evident in investment ties. Also crucial to this export growth has been Japan's role as their main external supplier of both machinery and fabrics. Their competitiveness, stemming from significantly lower labour costs (figure 3.1) has been enhanced by an open trade policy allowing free access to Japanese low-cost, high-quality fibre. Intra-industrial trade is thus substantial.

The same is not true of the more distant developed countries. Hong Kong, South Korea and Taiwan are the major suppliers to the United States' market but the United States is not as significant a supplier to them. These three LDCs also accounted for the whole of the EEC's textile deficit in 1976 (with a modest contribution from Brazil) (*Europe Information*, 1978, p. 48). So the European Industry Organization (CIRFS) felt justified in its 1976 study in arguing that if imports continued to grow, the European man-made fibre industry would be at great risk: 'in other words, if a polyester cotton shirt is imported there is not only a drop in production in the sector concerned but also in weaving, man-made fibre, spinning and petro-chemicals' (*Europe Information*, 1978, p. 35).[11] The MFA in this regard can be seen as an indication of the troubled and still incomplete integration of Japan with the Western market economies.

4.7.4 Offshore assembly

Offshore assembly involves the geographical relocation of the labour-intensive stages of apparel production to take advantage of lower labour costs in LDCs. The skill-intensive phases of fabric design, and sometimes also cutting, are retained at home and the sewing operation is subcontracted abroad. Once assembled, the final product is re-imported. The extension of this activity is fostered by 'value added tariffs' in many of the industrial countries, especially the United States, Netherlands and West Germany, which provide for partially duty-free re-import of such goods, i.e. the tariff on the finished good is applied only to the value added abroad as long as the components have originated in the importing country.[12] This development encourages internationalization of production and intra-industrial specialization. LDCs' lower labour costs are kept captive within established companies in developed countries rather than out of their bounds and threatening to push them out of business.

The MFA touches upon this sort of trade in Article 6.6:

> Consideration shall be given to special and differential treatment to re-imports into a participating country of textile products which that country has exported to another participating country for processing and subsequent re-importation, in the light of the special nature of such trade without prejudice to the provisions of Article 3.

So many disparate interests are at play that the wording is vague enough to give each importing country sufficient leeway to treat such re-imports according to whether domestic industry has emphasized offshore production or not. The bilateral agreements on quotas negotiated under the first MFA as well as the second one did not restrict goods processed abroad. Such trade, being tied to the production of firms operating in the importing countries, has enjoyed a sort of 'steered access'. Conflicts of interest have arisen, however, between management and labour unions among the EEC members which have structured the textile and clothing industry in different directions. West Germany and the Netherlands are the two members that have developed further along the lines of internationalized production. Most of this business is subcontracted to Eastern Europe and Yugoslavia and to a lesser extent to the Mediterranean countries. An extensive study of the West German industry at the Max Planck Institute showed that around 40 per cent of the country's textile firms and 70 per cent of the garment firms were engaged in production abroad (Froebel *et al.*, 1980, p. 111).[13] Not unnaturally, these countries have shown a more liberal orientation than the United Kingdom where industry followed exactly the opposite direction and concentrated investment in Britain itself, remaining comparatively higher-cost. Not unnaturally, the free circulation of offshore goods within the EEC became a contentious issue. In

1979 the Commission reached an agreement that re-imported goods would not be allowed to circulate freely and should be limited to the country and subcontracting the production (EEC Commission, Proposal to the Council, 1979), highlighting how uncommon the Common Market has been in this area.

Outward processing is a particular way of following global comparative advantages and international specialization, perhaps the only feasible way that the full impact of these principles can be allowed unfettered in North–South trade in manufactures. Such comparative advantages, being internalized by the firms, allow trade to be controlled by the interested parties in ways which have more in common with the principles of supply management than with arm's length rules. Given that the firms have a stake in ownership and the provision of components, imports are complementary to local production: they are not viewed unfavourably. With supply management, the traditional conflicts between exporting and importing countries will not arise. It is still, however, a very marginal trend in the textile and clothing sector. A decade after the launching of this scheme, only about one-tenth of American imports of textiles and apparel during the 1974–6 period were entered under Tariff Item 807.00, which is the United States' value added tariff. The 807.00 textile imports have mainly come from the Central American and Caribbean countries, nearly all being apparel from Mexico and Haiti (US, International Trade Commission, 1978, p. 29). In West Germany a similarly marginal proportion of imports is entered under the value added tariff provisions.

As outlined above, the extension of production along these lines may yet give rise to a different set of conflicts—North–North rather than North–South. Different stances over the extension of this production were one of the most contentious issues *within* the EEC during the internal negotiations to define a position for the renewal of MFA 3 (*The Financial Times*, 4 February 1980; 26 February 1982), with West Germany and the Netherlands pushing to retain their autonomy to operate such arrangements.

Another area of potential North–North conflict hinges on relations with Japan. At the time of the third renegotiation of the MFA, the EEC proposed to enforce a 10 per cent cutback on Hong Kong, Taiwan, South Korea and Macao's exports and as a quid pro quo offered to 'compensate' them for their cuts with outward processing deals (*The Financial Times*, 26 February 1982; *South*, February 1982), i.e. only if EEC fabrics were used to make clothing would quotas remain at the same level. In effect, the proposal amounted to a subtle attempt to erode the Japanese component of South-east Asia's exports and to widen the geographical expansion of European textile investment, so far almost entirely limited to Eastern Europe and the Mediterranean countries. The United States also made a similar proposal to Hong Kong (*The Financial Times*, 26 March 1982) in order to remove the trade imbalance. For LDCs these requests provided yet another confirmation that protectionism tends to gravitate towards sectors with bilaterally imbalanced trade, that is where trade has grown but intra-industry trade has lagged behind.

4.8 ALTERNATIVE FORMS OF PROTECTION: TARIFF INCREASES VERSUS QUOTAS

Hitherto we have been focusing on the North–South divide, or as A. J. Toynbee would have it, 'the West and the world', overlooking for the sake of clarity the conflicts of interest within each side. We will now very briefly dissect the complex set of interests on the LDCs' side that converge on the MFA and contribute to shaping it. But reference is needed first to the different implications of restricting trade by way of a tariff increase or a quantitative restriction.

An increase in tariffs drives a wedge between the domestic price and the world price of a good. If the tariff is increased on an MFN basis all foreign suppliers are given equal treatment and they continue to compete with each other on an equal footing. Yet, because the tariff has increased the price of the good in the domestic market, domestic producers have been shielded from the full blast of competition from lower-cost imports. Quota limitations also restrict foreign supply but in this case the market is rationed, each supplier receiving a specific share. Moreover, as the example of the butter dispute in Section 4.5 showed, a central criterion in the allocation of quotas is historical performance so that the effect is a relative safeguarding of acquired market shares. There is yet another way in which quota restrictions differ from tariffs. Consumer prices are indeed raised both with tariffs and quotas but with a different impact on the economic actors involved.

Economists have analysed the different effects of tariffs and quotas (Bergsten, 1975; Bhagwati, 1965; Hindley, 1980). When a tariff is imposed, an increased fiscal revenue accrues to the importing government. The market share of all the foreign suppliers taken together will be reduced by the effect of the tariff barrier; however, there is no a priori ceiling to the flow of trade but the demand for imports will adjust to the higher prices *ex post facto*. There is no rationing of market shares among the countries or firms involved. Unlike a tariff, a quota predetermines the level of import penetration. A quota can be either global or country-specific. A global quota will not discriminate among supplying countries as a country-specific one will. In this latter case it offers the possibility of discrimination by determining the amount that each country is allowed to sell. There are two possible ways of rationing the market— administration and control either at the import end or at the export end. Both will achieve the desired objective of restricting the supply of foreign goods but they are not equivalent in their distributional impact since the gains obtained from the restriction-induced price rise will accrue to different agents. The administration of the controls largely determines the distribution of the gains obtained and, as we shall see, the more tightly the buying or the selling agents are organized, the more clearly in their favour the distribution of the gains will be.[14]

If administration is carried out at the import end, the importing government will issue licenses to the importing firms. Without these licenses goods within the specified class and origin are refused entry. These licenses comprise a right to import particular goods from particular countries, allowing a source of gain to the firms that hold them since there is a difference in the price at which the exporters are willing to sell and the price at which the good is placed on the domestic market. This effect will be reinforced if importing power is concentrated in a few hands, reducing the chances that they will bid against each other.

On the other hand, if the quotas are enforced at the export end, they will operate as an export tax. Regardless of whether there is government involvement or not, firms must come together to agree on the allocation of the country's quota. Entry into the business ceases to be free and competition is decelerated. The exporting country thus gains a predominant share of the premium on quotas or price increases. In essence, restricting trade from the supply side allows exporters to maximize the premiums generated by the newly induced restriction and the relative scarcity; restricting trade by a similar amount from the demand side allows the importer to do so. Exporters have put the point succinctly:

> So long as you have a restraint agreement under which supply, that is export, is limited and demand continues high, then the price of the items we are exporting is bound to go up. Whether this is called a quota premium or is just an increase in price, the fundamental fact is that the normal laws of supply and demand are bound to operate. [*Textile Asia*, February 1976, p. 13.]

The MFA, as the LTA before it, acknowledged the right to administer the trade at the export end. The importing government admits goods provided they are covered by a copy of an export certificate issued by the exporting government. The certificate guarantees that the goods have been debited to the appropriate product category. By virtue of the government's undertaking to organize the export market by issuing licenses to firms, the export industry is induced into cartellization. If there is to be discipline, export market shares must be negotiated among the firms; and agreement must be reached beforehand to avoid shipments that might be refused entry. The government is also keen to guarantee a degree of order so as to maximize the use of the allocated quotas. Without an agreed order, if the shipment of certain products should exceed the ceiling and were refused access, waste of capital would result, increasing the risk for the firms involved and hindering their adaptability to fluctuating market conditions. A high rate of commercial collapses would ensue. On the other hand, if quotas remained unfilled, potential export opportunities and export earnings would be lost to the country. To avoid all this, what results is an *ad hoc* officially-policed cartellization which, owing to the dispersed production within the sector, is almost an imperative. Since firms must co-ordinate their action with more or less involvement from their governments, depending on the country in question, the result is a relative deceleration of the fierce competition inherent in the sector.

This point can be further illustrated by comparison with a similar situation in another industry, involving, however, only one country and a more concentrated export industry. In 1980, the European Community was concerned at the growth of Japanese machine-tool exports to it. In the first eight months of 1980, exports to West Germany and Great Britain were up 15 and 18 per cent respectively over the 1979 total. Exports to France had jumped 118 per cent and to Belgium 85 per cent. *The Financial Times* reported that the Ministry of International Trade and Industry (MITI) requested the Machinery Exporters Association, comprising sixty companies, to agree to a 'minimum price control'. Although there were at that time no plans to control volume, clearly it was to be expected that the voluntary price increase would result in a reduced demand for Japanese machine tools in Europe (*The Financial Times*, 3 December 1980). In this case no explicit rationing was envisaged, and competition for market-shares among the individual firm continued, though only at a higher price level, and naturally sustaining profits.

Heading off possible charges of disturbing markets or of dumping was a straightforward exercise in this case. Since only one country and its trade association were involved, self-regulation was feasible. Moreover, because of the technology and skilled labour used in this industry, the risk of substitution by other firms or countries was small. Unlike the case of textiles, here production facilities in un-restrained countries could not be set up promptly to fill the gap left by Japanese restraint. Textile exporters are not unaware of the unruly nature of their business and the role played by the MFA in this regard. The Chairman of a spinning and weaving mill in Bombay acknowledged that

> our post-war experience has clearly shown that there is no viable alternative to an internationally agreed and supervised system of textile trade. We all know that without the arrangement world trade in textiles might have been thrown into chaos. [International Federation of Cotton and Allied Textile Industries, Annual Conference, December 1976, p. 8.]

We have seen in Section 4.3 that what GATT means by market disruption is in fact the ability and the willingness of some foreign suppliers to sell goods at such low prices that they are difficult to match. Prima facie, then, an alternative to the MFA could have been a unilateral price increase. Had this been feasible it would have brought the added advantage of extra, effortless profits to the firms involved, derived from the difference in the price they were initially willing to sell at and the price that the importing government was prepared to admit as undisruptive. But as the history of commodity agreements has shown, ability to sustain a target price depends crucially on the ability to control the spread of alternative production sites. When substitution is possible, it leads to increased supplies from countries that will readily enter the market and undersell. To increase prices, then, when supply cannot be controlled, is self-defeating. The MFA, in this respect, gave to an industry not characterized by inelastic supply and therefore prone to congestion, the opportunity to restrict new entrants and thereby to sustain prices. By definition, the price of a cartellized good is raised compared to a situation of unrestricted supply. This was clear in the case of the Japanese machine-tools cited above when exporters were straightforwardly requested to raise their prices. But, as Brian Hindley has pointed out, in principle it makes little difference whether the road taken is an agreement to control the growth of volume as the MFA does, or a straightforward price increase, for the result in both cases is that the profit per unit sold is increased. Whether total profits increase or not will depend on the relative magnitude of each factor (Hindley, 1980, p. 321). If the price increase were large enough to more than offset the reduction in the volume of exports, the export industries would actually end up better-off than they were before the restrictions were introduced.

The Commonwealth Secretariat (1983, p. 164) has estimated that the MFA has raised prices of textiles and clothing by 15 to 40 per cent. Because of the characteristics of the industry (especially its supply elasticity and price competition), the success of the exporting industry in capturing as great a part as possible of this price increase depends on two levels of co-operation: firstly, among the individual firms of the export industry in each country and, secondly, close co-operation between these and their government. The closer the co-operation at both levels, the more selling power will be achieved. When the cotton restraints were first applied on Japan, in an effort to retain the benefits of the price increase at home rather than let them fall into the hands of the importers, MITI rejected applications for export licenses when offer prices were too low (Bergsten, 1975). In other words, there was a penalty for not quoting the 'right' price. Among LDCs, India's export control system also monitors offer prices. The significance of setting the 'right' price can also be seen to play at the import end. In Switzerland, where a system of import licenses is operated, the government may refuse to grant an import licence if the difference between the price of an imported good and the price of an equivalent domestic article exceeds a given margin (20 per cent for clothing). Therefore, should the exporters not be in a situation in which they can quote the 'right' price, the importer has been given the opportunity to raise the price unilaterally and to capture the gain. To be sure, governments in many LDCs may be unable or unwilling to bear the administrative burden of monitoring prices in several distant markets.

The prospect of sustaining profits is of significance in understanding why exporting countries have (given the alternatives) preferred the MFA to protective action under Article XIX. Should Article XIX be enforced, the exporting country would find itself faced with either a higher tariff on its exports (with the fiscal revenue accruing to the importing government), or alternatively with the enforcement of a global quota at the import end, the premium on quotas or price increase thus being captured by the importers rather than the exporters. Potential exporters eager to sell would have to go in search of the importer with a quota right. At that point they would bid against each other, pushing their offer prices down. The goods, however, would still command a higher price from consumers, yet the gain, rather than being captured by the exporters, would go to those on the importing side who hold the rights to import.

Prima facie, then, if the alternative to acceptance of the MFA is, or is perceived to be, some increased protection by recourse to Article XIX, exporters will prefer to negotiate an export restraint. Moreover, the weapons of retaliation and compensation envisaged in Article XIX are virtually irrelevant for the exporters involved. While under the quota system they are given some financial compensation for the limitations on market access, the sort of compensation envisaged by Article XIX in the form of retaliation (withdrawal of a concession by the damaged exporting country) or the right to request a tariff compensation (an equivalent tariff concession on another product of interest to the country) does not provide nearly the same consolation. In the first place, an equivalent concession on a different product would increase market access for an industry other than the particular export business suffering from the limitations. The compensatory tariff concession accrues to other firms with no consolation to the firms whose production had been geared to the now shrinking export market. Moreover, from the point of view of the government of the exporting country with an eye on the overall balance of payments, if an equivalent concession is to be meaningful, other export industries must be ready to fill the gap left by the reduced earnings from textile exports. This may prove difficult for LDCs with limited export options. To put it in an extreme form, if, say, 40 per cent of a country's export receipts are provided by the textile sector (as in the case of Hong Kong), how can a compensatory concession on, say, canned tuna fish, be genuinely equivalent? It could be argued that a country faced with restrictions on its textile exports will be compensated because it is induced to diversify its exports. There is no reason to dispute the diversification effect,[15] but to operate this reconversion will take time, and in the meantime the country is forced to forgo a part of its export receipts as a result of the restraints imposed on textiles. So the direct and immediate compensation provided by the un-ostensible cartellization that the MFA brings about is, *given the alternatives*, an attraction to the exporters.

The second defensive weapon envisaged by GATT's rules is retaliation by the injured country in the form of the withdrawal of a concession previously benefiting the protectionist offender. Again, this does not offer any com-pensation to the injured firms and from the point of view of the government it is not always in the position in which an increase in the protection afforded to an imported good will be a rational or even practicable economic choice. There would be little justification, for example, to increase the protection on an industrial input that the country does not produce domestically and therefore needs to buy abroad, since it would only lead to higher production costs. It is plausible that retaliation could hurt the victim more than the victimizer. The whole tariff bargaining procedure of GATT, with its retaliatory and compensatory weapons, rests too strongly on the assumption of self-contained economies with ample freedom for manœuvre in concession-swapping. This image does not fit LDCs. It may fit developed countries better, but even for them the image needs to be reformulated, as I argued in Chapter 3.

The Hong Kong trade publication, *Textile Asia*, noted that export control under the MFA 'is a small partial compensation for the fact that we are accepting a restriction on our trade' (February 1976, p. 67). Should the export control system be changed to an import control system, the importer would benefit from the competition among potential exporters and would thus be able 'to squeeze out the lowest quotations' (*Textile Asia*, February 1976, p. 67).

To summarize, the implementation of the MFA has induced a situation of relative scarcity. Tight restraint limits have transformed an elastic foreign supply into a relatively less elastic one and therefore reduced the impact of competition from low-cost imports in the developed markets. But by granting the sellers the possibility of organizing themselves, it has also blunted the competition among them. The operation of the price mechanism has been eroded in an intrinsically price-competitive industry, thus transforming its market structure.

As described in Chapter 3, in the majority of industrial sectors this transformation of the market structure away from price competition and towards concentration had operated by other means. Next only to agri-culture, the textile sector is more prone to congestion and price competition than any other industrial activity, and therefore when the tightening of trade became necessary government involvement as well as sanction by GATT were required. Concentrated industries are comparatively more able to arrange quotas and agreements at a prior stage, that of production, whereas competition among unconcentrated industries will spill over onto trade. One could argue that the more unconcentrated the sector, the more overarching the framework required to regulate its trade. Textile trade therefore needed supervision and enforcement by an international institution.

4.8.1 Balance of interests among LDCs

In the same way as the MFA restricts access among firms within an exporting country, it restricts the entry of new countries. Access is no longer free; it must be negotiated. The MFA has thus controlled 'global mushrooming'. It imposes a situation of relative scarcity but not all exporting countries are affected in the same way. The exporting countries are only at a superficial level a bloc. They have, to be sure, a minimum common denominator—right of market access—that keeps them together for certain issues and at certain stages. But, at other stages, their interests may be opposed. At least three groups of countries can be distinguished:[16] (a) the so-called 'dominant suppliers', Hong Kong, Taiwan and South Korea; (b) the other Asian suppliers; and (c) the smaller, more marginal suppliers.

Quota protection makes competition for a share of the market a zero sum game. The 'dominant suppliers' will be interested in at least preserving their historical market shares from potential newcomers. If the growth of their export volume is reduced they will seek compensation in rising prices. For this to be feasible new entrants must be monitored so that they cannot fill the gap left by their own self-restraint.

In the 'dominant suppliers', the quota allocation for most products is an effective ceiling on export growth, that is, supply is restricted while demand continues high—albeit with seasonal variations. Therefore, sellers are placed in a strong position to control the market. In Hong Kong, Taiwan, and South Korea exporting is so lucrative that quota allocations command a premium and are traded among firms. In Hong Kong a fully-fledged quota market has developed with quota brokers, known as 'quota farmers'. These are individuals who are no longer manufacturers or exporters but who have retained their historical quotas and who now deal in them.

The smaller, newly aspiring Asian suppliers, in contrast, are keen to acquire a slice of the market. Despite very low wages, they may not be able to meet the competition from the large exporters. The quota system therefore shelters them against these competitors and may in some cases provide a further incentive for export growth. As a result of tight quotas on the 'dominant suppliers' and the premium on quotas, firms have shifted their trading connections to a base in neighbouring countries. Production facilities have been set up in this fashion in Indonesia, Macao, Thailand, Malaysia, etc. (*Textile Asia*, April 1976, pp. 74–5). With the objective of attracting this business, Sri Lanka implemented an export-processing zone in 1977 and clothing exports to the EEC jumped from a very low base by nearly 1000 per cent over a two-year period.

Finally there come the more marginal suppliers where the inclination to export is not as strong as in East Asia. The quota allocations for these countries remain largely unfulfilled; they carry no premium and therefore cannot be bought or sold. World Bank research on Colombian textile exports by David Morawetz reports that, but for a few product categories, quotas remained under-utilized and even when they were fulfilled exporting was not such a profitable business 'as to make quotas worth fighting for' (Morawetz, 1982, p. 125). Some delegations to GATT admit that the MFA does not restrict their own country's trade but assures it of a market share; they have also reported that frequently MFA negotiations are requested by domestic firms. Similarly, buyers for an American firm stated that almost all the garments they ordered in Colombia could be bought 10 to 30 per cent less expensively in East Asia. All the same, the company wanted to do business in the country, 'to ensure a foothold should there be a cut in European import quotas for apparel from East Asia or should a war break out in Korea again' (Morawetz, 1982, p. 30).

4.9 CONCLUSIONS

This chapter has examined the structural forces that led to the emergence of the MFA and aimed to demonstrate why the textile and clothing sector, unable to follow the GATT's standard mode of operation, required the GATT to perform its antithetical role, to enforce protectionism. In the first place, the production of the textile sector has predominantly been organized nationally rather than internationally. There are, however, other sectors that, despite operating nationally, such as the ship-building and steel sector (Strange, 1979), have not required a multilateral framework to manage trade. One must therefore look for other forces operating in the textile sector as well as its mode of operation. In developed countries two influences played a key role in spurring protectionist policies. In the United States, the cotton industry was inevitably affected by the impact of agricultural policies aimed at increasing farm incomes. Domestic support prices for cotton since 1955 meant that domestic mills were having to pay higher than world prices for the cotton they consumed, which naturally led to a situation in which textile goods produced in the United States were more costly than their world counterparts. The pressure of lower-cost cotton imports therefore grew until 1966, when a programme was devised to divert farmers from cotton to other crops. In this sense the LTA was a direct offspring of the 1955 GATT waiver that allowed the United States to operate its farm programme. At the same time, protection for cotton products contributed to the substitution for man-made fibres.

By 1965, when the switch from cotton to man-made fibres was in full swing, the chemical and the chemical fibres corporations predominating in each national market generated a suction movement over the clothing sector—the main outlet for their fibres. It was not difficult for the highly concentrated chemical fibre corporations to play a key role in support of protectionism and to drag along downstream clothing firms whose output is typically less concentrated. Courtaulds' 1981 *Annual Report* (p. 2) acknowledged: 'We welcome the assurance of the government that it will seek a renewal of the Multi-Fibre Arrangement on tough terms . . . the current MFA is too short term and insufficiently comprehensive to allow adjustment in the developed countries without unacceptable social strains'.

While these two powerful driving forces operated in developed countries, attempting to obstruct access to markets which would make comparative advantage operate, numerous LDCs, bent on the accelerated expansion of their textile and clothing industries, produced a 'global mushrooming' of the textile industry either by processing their own cotton or, as in South Asia, through export-orientated policies coupled with closer links with Japan as a supplier of marketing networks, fabrics, fibres, machinery or capital. The expansion of the Japanese foreign investment and trading networks is a factor operating in the evolution of the MFA. Whereas American and European multinational firms expanded in industries characterized by oligopolistic market structures in both home and host countries, Japanese manufacturing investment followed a somewhat different pattern. It has invested more frequently in standardized goods produced by competitive industries, and as such has contributed to the build-up of the textile and clothing industries in its neighbouring countries. As shown by Ozawa's study of Japanese multi-nationals, the firms were predominantly small and medium-sized, substantially assisted by the ready-made marketing network of the big Japanese trading companies, concerned with the loss of business as a result of quotas on products made in Japan. Hong Kong firms have been following in Japan's footsteps and also expanding in neighbouring countries.

The industry nevertheless remained fiercely competitive, and it was precisely this feature that led to the need for an international formula to regulate trade. The fact that production was scattered among infinite factories dispersed in innumerable countries meant that trade management required a global solution. Textile trade regulations are special in that they are an international arrangement with the backing not only of governments but also of an international institution. Trade restrictions in steel, cars, etc. have not needed an international formula because they are not such fiercely competitive industries: market sharing arrangements are relatively simpler exercises because of the reduced number of participants, both at government and firm level. Competition may be fierce, for example, in the market for video cassette recorders, but it is restricted to just a few companies and their home governments. However difficult it may be to reach an agreement, once it is reached there is no risk that it will be undermined by competition from outsiders because of the entry barriers to the industry itself. Dramatically opposite is the case of the textile and clothing sector (with the exclusion of man-made fibre production), where innumerable firms scattered across the globe compete to produce mostly standardized, low-technology products. Product differentiation in the way of branded goods, a response by big companies in developed countries to the fierce competition in the industry, is an increasingly manifest trend. Yet, especially at the lower end of the market, price competition persists and sustains the continued need for a global framework of trade regulations under GATT's umbrella. In sum, GATT was involved in administering a derogation from its rules, precisely because of the openness of the market and the consequent room for continued price competition. Textile firms in developed countries and their governments saw the need to put a brake on it, in order to arrest further polarization, or 'market disruption'. So many conflicting trends had of necessity to be articulated into a multilateral formula.

Paradoxically , the fierce competition in the industry at a global level makes it in principle the sort of industry for which GATT was conceived: a sector in which market access was being gained through price competition—comparative advantages held by competing firms in different countries. But the character of world trade was no longer essentially tied to price competition. It was precisely because textiles retained price-competitive features that it came to be removed from the normal *modus operandi*. The allocation of quotas has blunted the operation of the price mechanism in an intrinsically price-competitive industry, thus transforming the market structure of the sector. In this sense the MFA, as the LTA before it, are an aberration from the principles GATT was conceived for, though, as we have tried to demonstrate, the unconcentrated nature of the textile business made strict trade regulations imperative. The quota system, moreover, has created vested interests in LDCs. It has restricted the access of new firms to an industry which had previously been extremely easy to enter but which offered comparatively low returns; in the absence of the MFA the sector would most probably have consisted of a larger number of more competitive firms. Quota limitations have also made it possible to sustain prices.

As regards the conflict of interests among the LDCs, the quota system has created a new set of contradictions. On the one hand, it carves out a market share for those countries which cannot compete with South-east Asia either on prices or trading organization. At the same time it preserves the historical market shares of the dominant suppliers, shielding them from newcomers. It is difficult to ascertain which of these potentially opposite directions may be the stronger since we do not have a non-MFA world economy to compare the existing system with, but in any case the MFA has created vested interests in LDCs, contributing further to its resilience.

NOTES

1. With similar intellectual roots but on opposite grounds, the representative of India at the 9th session of the Contracting Parties in 1954 had claimed that 'equal treatment is equitable only among equals' and that therefore the rule of reciprocity in tariff negotiations should be derogated for LDCs.
2. Again, a line of reasoning sharing intellectual roots with Prebisch's questioning of the principles of comparative advantages.
3. LDCs' safeguard action has been mainly induced by balance of payments problems and so taken under Article XVIII.
4. South Korea lodged a complaint in GATT and subsequently an agreement was reached whereby Britain removed the import restriction in exchange for self-imposed restrictions at the export end. Self-imposed restrictions are known as voluntary export restraints or 'VERs'. Section 8 of this chapter will attempt to explain why exporters opt for self-control rather than face controls at the import end.
5. Anticipating the conclusion to be reached shortly in the text, the ground for this discrimination was implicitly the wide wage disparities between developed and less developed countries (See Figure 3.1). 'Disruption' emerges when trade takes place between countries of dissimilar cost structures, as List pointed out.
6. Liberal in the sense that neither the United States nor Britain applied quantitative restrictions over and above tariffs: tariffs were applied on all suppliers in the United States and, in Britain, on non-Commonwealth suppliers since the institution of Imperial Preference in 1932.
7. Invocation of Article XXXV was renounced during 1963–4 when Japan shifted from its transitional status within the IMF to full membership.
8. Dam reported that in the first three years of the operation of the LTA, American restraint orders affected imports from seventeen countries and a total of forty-nine out of sixty-four product categories—a far greater coverage than had been expected (Dam, 1970, p. 308).
9. See Dohlman (1985) on the Nordic input into the MFA.
10. The footwear industry is also labour-intensive but overall it is a much smaller industry in most countries. In Britain it employs less than one-tenth of the labour that is employed in the textile sector and is characterized by small, one-plant firms (Cable, 1983).
11. It should be noted that although the United States is the major fibre producer, Europe has not been as worried about competition from the United States as from Asia. The reason is related to the fact that, except for a short period in 1979–80, the trade balance in textiles with the United States has traditionally been in 'substantial surplus' (EEC Commission, Communication to the Council, *Report on Two Years' Operation of the Multifibre Agreement*, Brussels, 1979, p. 14). That temporary deficit nevertheless provoked a strong reaction from European industry and quotas were subsequently applied under GATT's Article XIX. (*The Financial Times*, 20 April 1980). The application exempted EFTA countries and all countries with which the EEC had previous bilateral agreements.
12. See Chapter 3.

13. Despite so many firms being involved abroad, the proportion of offshore processed goods over total imports is still a marginal 10 per cent.
14. If a quota is fixed in global terms (i.e. with no predetermined country share), it will be filled on a first-come, first-served basis. So this alternative is equivalent to placing the administration of quotas at the import end (described below). It increases buying-power at the expense of selling-power because exporters bid against each other, competing for prompt arrival at port as well as on offer prices.
15. Except on the grounds that it is suspiciously self-serving. It seems to be telling LDCs: 'The defence of narrow individual interests may be inflicting pain on you but it is in your own best interest to take the flogging.'
16. Even this classification may be too aggregative, since the weight of the textile industry and the way exports are organized varies widely from country to country.

5 The oscillations of regional economic integration in Latin America: LAFTA-LAIA

5.1 INTRODUCTION

In the preceding chapter we have looked at LDCs' exports, taking a sectoral approach and a South–North direction. This is a way in which most LDCs plugged into international trade, the Asian countries being the forerunners in manufactures. While they took the lead in the efforts to obtain wider access to the markets of developed countries, the Latin American countries grappled with devices to boost their mutual trade. A particular set of problems also arose in this context. Co-operative ventures here proved extremely difficult to mount, let alone to operate successfully; but the gist of the story is different from the one in the previous chapter. Here I will be taking a regional rather than a sectoral view, and a South–South direction instead of a North–South.

During colonial times, North–South channels of trade, communications and transport were developed, while restrictions were imposed on South–South trade and communications. Most LDCs have been keen to boost South–South trade as a way of removing this South–North straightjacket, of diversifying their trade and of countering the sort of biases that have been described in their trade with developed countries. Institutional arrangements were sought, largely at a regional level and among neighbouring countries.[1] Their efforts may have been disappointing but they were not an utter failure. Looking at matters in the aggregate, Keesing (1977) showed that the exports of manufactures from LDCs have been mainly absorbed by other LDCs. In a less aggregate picture, Stewart (1976) showed that South–South trade has been mostly regional rather than inter-regional; it has been confined almost exclusively to the same geographical area. Of the Middle East's total manufactured exports to other LDCs, 56 per cent were absorbed in the same region; in Asia 67 per cent, 73 per cent in Africa and for Latin America, a high of 96 per cent.

The desire to boost regional trade emerged in Latin America in the late-1950s, before it did in other regions of the less developed world. Latin America was by then in broad terms relatively more industrialized than other regions and it had a longer history of political independence and mutual trade. It had for long been interested in the creation of special schemes to promote regional trade. During the preparatory sessions for the Havana Conference for the ITO, Brazil, as a representative of the Latin American countries, had pressed for the right of LDCs to form regional preference areas without having to go so far as to create an orthodox customs union or a free trade area (Kock, 1969, p. 245). The Havana Charter incorporated provisions for preferential agreements in Article XV but the General Agreement did not include this article and banned new preferences among its signatories. It was not until the 1950s that the ideas on regional integration were given a more concrete shape.

In chronological terms, the Latin American Free Trade Area, set up in February 1960, was the first integration scheme agreed by LDCs. The antecedents of the East African Community date back to 1917 and hence to colonial instigation; only in 1967 did an agreement emerge from the constitutionally independent governments. The Central American Common Market (CACM) was concluded shortly after LAFTA in December 1960; but military conflicts among its members and the threat of American intervention have interfered with its evolution, making an appraisal nearly impracticable. Moreover, only one member of the CACM, Nicaragua, was a GATT signatory, so that the GATT was not able to play as active a role as the Economic Commission for Latin America (ECLA). LAFTA was not only the first trading arrangement among LDCs; it was also the first, as well as the last, that made an effort to comply with the GATT norms. Subsequently initiatives tended, on the one hand, to be more openly heterodox and, on the other, to take up ideas first tried by LAFTA.

5.2 FACTORS LEADING TO REGIONAL INTEGRATION

Although the Latin Americans had lobbied at Havana to obtain the right to grant each other preferential concessions, the General Agreement specifically banned any future preferences. Only Chile and Brazil had attended the Geneva Conference that led to the setting up of the GATT. The initiative was kept dormant until the end of the 1950s, when three factors converged to change the situation: anxieties about the trade implications of the EEC, the declining trend in Latin American trade and the catalytic role played by the structuralist school of economic thought that sprang from the work of ECLA.[2]

Firstly, towards the end of the 1950s, it seemed that a trend towards the parcelling out of the world market into regional blocs would grow. In Europe the European Free Trade Area (EFTA) was set up as a response to the EEC; in Latin America the creation of the EEC generated a 'demonstration effect' whereby governments were led to believe that the example should be followed. Moreover, the Treaty of Rome contemplated the granting of trade preferences to former European colonies (Treaty of Rome, Part IV, Articles 131–6), so there was also considerable concern at the increasing influence of regionalism and at the creation of a potential trade bloc that excluded Latin America. This concern was repeatedly voiced in GATT (GATT, SR 15/15, 1959, p. 142; L/805/Rev. 1, 1958; SR 18/4, 1961, p. 50; L/1902, 1962).

A second factor was the interest of Argentina, Brazil, Chile and Uruguay in preserving their shrinking mutual trade in primary commodities which was covered by sixteen bilateral treaties. These countries had been trading with one another since the 1930s on the basis of special tariff preferences. These preferences were incorporated when drafting the General Agreement as exceptions to Article I since Brazil and Chile were among GATT's founding parties (General Agreement, Annex E).

Beside this preferential system of tariffs, the countries concerned had employed bilateral exchange and trade controls since the 1930s. For example, Brazil would allocate foreign exchange for imports of wheat from Argentina and not for similar imports from third countries. Argentina reciprocated with comparable import and foreign exchange regulations (Dell, 1966, p. 26).

The use of direct controls over and above tariff preferences was partly the result of participating in GATT. The tariff preferences in force in 1947 were granted exception from the MFN clause, but, as had been anticipated, the tariff bargaining at GATT rounds reduced the margin of preference[3] that not only Brazil and Chile (founding parties), but also Uruguay and Peru (which joined GATT in 1949 and 1950 respectively) applied to imports from their neighbouring partners (Dell, 1966, p. 26). From the mid-1950s, however, with the return to convertibility in Europe coupled with the greater weight of IMF payment rules, controls over trade and payments began to be dismantled as well.

Although the margin of preference was not eroded in Argentina, other factors worked against it. From 1945 to 1955 the Peronist government had pursued strongly nationalist foreign economic policies and at the time of the Havana Charter had led the opposition to it on the grounds that it was an 'imperialist instrument' (*Hechos e Ideas*, Vol. 12, January 1948, p. 267). Perón was particularly opposed to the restrictions on state trading and the ban on regional preferences. On regional preferences, the monthly *Hechos e Ideas*, a mouthpiece for the Peronist government, pointed out:

> Latin America cannot give up this elementary right to economic association or integration equivalent to the right enjoyed by the United States of North America in the political terrain. These agreements are justified by the need to complement basic production, widen markets for industrial develop- ment and the defence against foreign economic might. Regional prefer- ences are a first step towards a Latin American customs union that should one day compensate in the economic terrain the disadvantages of excessive and misguided political disaggregation. [*Hechos e Ideas*, Vol. 12, January 1948, p. 273.]

The military takeover that ousted Perón in 1955 dismantled the state trading corporation and moved quickly to bring foreign economic policy in line with multilateral requirements. Raúl Prebisch, then head of the Economic Commission for Latin America, was called in to advise and, following his recommendations (República Argentina, *Plan de reestablecimiento económico*, 1956, p. 48), Argentina joined the World Bank and the IMF. While payments were very soon reorganized to adjust to multilateral rules, the tariff structure took longer. Although Prebisch had not included accession to GATT in his advice, an observer was sent to Geneva to follow the work of GATT in 1958; two years later the government formally requested to open negotiations for accession but these were not completed until the end of the Kennedy Round in 1967, by which time LAFTA was already in being.

Together with the dismantling and erosion of bilateral arrangements, trade among the Latin American countries began to decline. In 1953 exports of Latin American countries to one another reached a record high of 12.1 per cent of total exports and by 1961 they had declined to 7.1 per cent. In absolute terms, the highest dollar total of Latin American regional trade was reached in 1955 and, from that point up to 1961, while trade among Latin American countries declined by over 25 per cent, their imports from the rest of the world grew by more than 20 per cent (Dell, 1966, pp. 26–7). The entire decline in regional trade was concentrated among the countries that subsequently joined LAFTA, and particularly among Argentina, Brazil, Chile and Uruguay, who had reduced their controls over trade and payments and were shifting to multilateralism.

Of the total decline in regional trade amounting to $200 million, that of Argentina, Brazil, Uruguay and Chile accounted for 90 per cent (Table 5.1). This drastic drop in intra-regional trade at a time when imports from the rest of the world were expanding was seen to be a reflection of the shift from bilateral to multilateral policies of trade and payments. Concerned by this trend, the countries got together in 1958 to discuss means of restoring and preserving the trade that had hitherto been carried out under bilateral arrangements. Brazil, Chile and Uruguay were by then contracting parties to GATT, whereas Argentina was negotiating its accession; their initiative was conditioned to take into account the requirements of multilateralism as set down by GATT. Article XXIV of GATT allowed two types of exceptions to the application of MFN treatment—a free-trade area or a customs union. According to Article XXIV, a free-trade area is a grouping of two or more countries, 'in which the duties and other restrictive regulations of commerce ... are eliminated on substantially all the trade between the constituent territories in products originating in such territories' (Article XXIV.8 b). A customs union must, over and above that, establish a common external tariff. Since this required closer co-ordination of foreign economic policies than Argentina, Brazil, Chile and Uruguay were prepared to accept, they

Table 5.1 Latin American trade, 1955–61 (in $m)

	1955	1961	Decrease
Exports of all Latin American countries to one another	770	570	200
Exports of LAFTA to one another	508	299	209
—of which Argentina	190	100	90
Brazil	145	95	50
Uruguay	31	6	25
Chile	58	35	23

Source: Dell (1966, p.27).

embarked instead on the idea of a free-trade area in accordance with Article XXIV.

5.2.1 The role of ECLA

Just as a particular set of beliefs had in its time inspired the inception of the GATT, economic doctrine, though of a different kind, also played a role in the creation of LAFTA. This leads us to the third factor that influenced Latin American integration. Import substitution and regional integration were among ECLA's central tenets in the area of international trade from the very outset. The *Economic Survey for Latin America* for 1949 called for initiatives to increase intra-Latin American trade. But with the relative boom in Latin American trade which accompanied the Korean war, governments did not include the search for such initiatives among their top priorities. Their attitude was soon reversed with the decline in the growth rate of exports which took place in the years 1953 to 1955. This was the kind of politically favourable climate in which ECLA was able to step up its lobbying among the regional governments.

The motives for advocating integration were naturally very much a part of the comprehensive critique of international trade being elaborated at the time. In ECLA's thinking, regional integration was crucial to obtain the economies of large-scale production offered by the technological development of modern industry. Without access to external markets, it would not be possible to sustain the growth of import substitution industries. Output curves rose rapidly when imports were first being replaced, but stagnated when further growth became dependent, firstly on the growth of domestic demand and, ultimately, on the growth of domestic income. At this point the level of investment was reduced and industries reached 'precocious maturity' (Hirschman, 1971, p. 98). In the first, 'easy' stage of import substitution, lower duties for machinery imports or preferential exchange rates made for lavish orders. Thus, the new industries, deceived as to the real size of the market, soon tended to find themselves saddled with diseconomies of scale and unused capacity. ECLA pointed out that access to foreign markets would reverse the situation and allow economies of scale. But since Latin America's industrial goods were uncompetitive in world markets, regional economic integration was the way to 'spark off' the beginning of an export drive which would avoid stagnation in the long run.[4]

Since it was an offspring of the comprehensive critique of international trade, the proposal reflected a search for original criteria instead of strict acceptance of Article XXIV. Two main points of divergence from Article XXIV were envisaged. In the first place, the proposal envisaged what was in essence the establishment of a preferential trade area. In an initial ten-year stage, the aim was to secure a reduction in the average level of tariffs with the abolition of tariffs on as many items as possible. More orthodox objectives, such as full liberalization of 'substantially all the trade' or the setting-up of a common external tariff would be made to wait for a later phase. The second deviation from Article XXIV was a proposal to institute differential treatment to take into account the diverse stages of development attained by member countries. ECLA proposed two kinds of differential tariff treatment. On the one hand, countries in the group that were relatively less developed would be allowed to retain higher degrees of protection. On the other hand, the more advanced countries would grant non-reciprocal concessions to the less advanced of the group (ECLA, 1959 and Salgado, 1979). We have seen that non-reciprocity and preferential treatment were also reforms proposed in the GATT ambit (Chapter 2).

Sustained by faith in industrialization and scepticism about the un-regulated play of market forces, 'the doctrine of integration elevated to the multinational plane the thesis that economic development is impossible without industrialization' (Wionczek, 1966, p. 3). Integration extended the policy of import substitution from a national to a continental scale. The fundamental aim was to undertake a more advanced stage of import sub-stitution. The process of industrialization could be deepened if it were not duplicated from country to country as if these were 'watertight compart-ments' (Prebisch, *et al.*, 1966, p. 290). The established consumer goods industries could reduce their high costs and the capital goods sector could develop. Trade protection was to be maintained *vis-à-vis* extra-regional producers. Capital goods production was an infant industry and scarce foreign exchange could not be squandered on consumer goods that were already locally supplied.

5.2.2 The battle of ideas: complementarity versus competition

In ECLA's thinking, economic integration was designed to work via the economies of scale that would be achieved. Countries would complement each other's markets and hence import substitution would become more efficient through the enlargement of the sheltered market. Latin America, it was maintained, was producing much less than it could, owing to the fragmentation of what could and should be a single large market. A large market was 'indispensable if production was to be efficient and low cost, even in the most densely populated countries of Latin America' (Prebisch *et al.*, 1966, p. 290).

Complementarity would be based on established industrial capacity as well as on future investments. Economic planning would serve as a guide in the setting up of complementarity agreements, 'but it would be private enterprise that in the final issue would decide which industries were to be established, in which countries they were to be installed, and what degree of specialisation was to be attained' (ECLA, 1959, p. 22).

Orthodoxy was against ECLA's scheme, despite the latter's professed alliance on private enterprise. It maintained that industrial inefficiency was a consequence of excessive protection: the price mechanism had not been allowed to operate at its fullest. Consequently, the problem could only be solved by the freer interplay of market forces and the exposure of Latin American industries to the invigorating and cleansing effects of global competition. The complementarity of Latin American economies advocated by ECLA was believed to be damaging because it interfered further with the market and hindered imports from cheaper sources of supply outside the LAFTA arrangements, giving rise to further inefficiencies. The most influential writing on the subject at the time explained the merits of customs unions in terms of the balance between trade creation and trade diversion (Viner, 1950). It held that trade diversion (which should be avoided) occurred when a country imported from a higher-cost source after union than it had before union. Trade creation (which should be encouraged) occurred when there was a shift in the location of industries from high- to low-cost areas within the union.

By then, a leading figure in the free-trade school in Latin America was Brazilian Roberto Oliveira Campos. Campos was Ambassador to GATT and had co-authored the Haberler Report. Second in prominence was Argentinian Robert Alemann, then Minister for the Economy. At the GATT Ministerial Meeting of November 1961, Alemann delivered a speech referring exclusively to the need to liberalize trade in agricultural products and made no reference to preferential access for manufactures, although the subject was mentioned in the speeches of most other LDCs (GATT, Proceedings, 1961).

Neo-classicals were intent on following the guidelines for a free-trade area approved in Article XXIV.

It is fundamental to an understanding of LAFTA's fate to see the sort of compromise that brought the Treaty of Montevideo into being. The structuralists expected industrial complementarity to encourage import substitution on a greater scale, providing a renewed impetus for industrial growth. Although the desired end-result would be increased specialization, it would be reached through negotiation and not by the indiscriminate release of market forces. At the other end of the spectrum, free traders advocated economic integration as a means of furthering the subordination of local industries to the logic of global comparative advantages—an initial step towards greater liberalization *vis-à-vis* the rest of the world. Freer intra-regional trade should force industries to lower costs or to disappear should they fail to achieve this, as demand would then be redirected to cheaper suppliers. Free traders do not see such a process as wasteful, as the structuralist theorists do:

> For free trade-minded economists, the size of the market avaiable to a country's export industry is a share of the international market which can be increased only by that industry's capacity to lower costs and improve its competitive power. Thus the country's capacity to improve efficiency and reduce costs in its export production is a prior condition for taking advantage of the scope for the economies of large scale production offered by international trade. [Myint, 1969, p. 18.]

In the structuralist conception, freer intra-Latin American trade would lead to a desirable situation in which countries would decide their imports not on the basis of given price signals but on the possibility of placing with their suppliers industrial exports which might initially lack competitiveness in the international market. For example, Colombia would reduce car imports from cheaper extra-regional sources to buy from Mexico in exchange for office machines that might also have to be manufactured at higher than international prices in the first stages of the economic union. Among LDCs, some degree of trade diversion was not only unavoidable but also necessary: it would gradually lead to fuller utilization of resources and continental specialization.

> If a country imported from other Latin American countries goods which it had formerly received from the rest of the world . . . its ability to finance imports with additional exports would be a decisive factor in the smooth operation of the common market. It is also essential that the country thus receiving imports of manufactured goods should be able to cover them with its own exports of industrial products as well as primary commodities. [ECLA, 1959, p. 21.]

This contrast in the approach of structuralists and free traders towards the role of the international market constitutes the fundamental disagreement from which all their other differences spring. Although the contrast may have been presented here in an extreme form, it is indeed no mere technical dispute but one that has aroused impassioned political controversy.[5] Furthermore, it was at the base of the intense diplomatic negotiations that were held to accommodate the competing projects from 1957 to 1960; it was also at the core of the many policy fluctuations that arose from then on, as structuralists and free traders succeeded each other in national bureaucracies. Both lines of thought shaped the Treaty of Montevideo in 1960, providing the framework for LAFTA. 'The Latin American Free Trade Area thus came into being as a hybrid' (Finch, 1982, p. 209).

ECLA's original proposal for the construction of a preferential trade area gave way to the free-trade area initiative put forward by Argentina, Brazil, Chile and Uruguay, which received the backing of GATT and the government of the United States. The GATT Secretariat considered that, of the two competing projects, the one delineated by ECLA entailed the risk of remaining in the preferential phase without any guarantee of moving in the direction of a free-trade area later on, since it offered a plan of liberalization for the first stage only. GATT sent a representative to the negotiations. When the free-trade area proposal reached a winning position at a meeting in November 1959, the GATT representative went on record to express his pleasure, 'that the views of the Latin American countries were very close to those held by GATT' (ECLA, 1959, p. 123), and then went on to stress that 'the final aim should always be a competitive market without restrictions' (ECLA, 1959, p. 123). It so happened that the notion of 'market disruption' was simultaneously being inscribed in GATT to arrest competition between LDCs and developed countries.[6]

At the same meeting the representative of the United States emphasized 'the unsatisfactory nature' of the scheme presented by ECLA. The United States Embassy in Brazil had been blunter the year before: 'The United States would gladly see the establishment in Latin America of customs unions or free trade areas which satisfy criteria in Article XXIV of the General Agreement on Tariffs and Trade' (ECLA, 1959, p. 123). Thus, in the course of the negotiations ECLAs' programme, lacking substantive governmental support, was tailored to follow the provisions of Article XXIV more closely. Yet the industrial complementarity agreements that ECLA had postulated were incorporated in Articles 16 and 17 of the Treaty of Montevideo. Differential treatment of the relatively less developed countries of the group, in the form of special non-reciprocal concessions to be granted to them, were also included in Article 32. This departure in commercial policy on the principle of reciprocity and MFN treatment to correspond with levels of development among Latin American countries was also part of the debate in the GATT ambit. In 1961 Chile's representative to GATT, Fernando García Oldini, proposed 'giving concessions to the LDCs without compensation' (GATT, SR 18/4, p. 52). Part IV of the General Agreement subsequently enshrined the principle in Article XXXVI (paragraph 8) and in 1971 a waiver of Article I was agreed to implement the General System of Preferences (GSP) (see Chapter 2.)[7]

5.3 POLICY INSTRUMENTS

The Treaty of Montevideo provided three means of removing tariffs. Tariff reduction, according to Articles 4, 5, 6 and 7, partly followed the product-by-product GATT procedure and partly the traditional across-the-board formula for the establishment of a free-trade area. A third mode of liberalization for industrial goods was introduced by Articles 15 and 16. To take these in turn: firstly, in a GATT-style way, negotiations would take place annually for tariff reductions in each country's national schedules. All members undertook to reduce duties and charges equivalent to no less than 8 per cent of the weighted average applicable to third countries, until these were eliminated for 'substantially all' its imports from LAFTA. [Article 5.] Each country could select the products on which it was prepared to offer concessions on an MFN basis, and should it wish to withdraw concessions at a later stage, it was obliged to negotiate adequate compensation. As in GATT, the result would be that each contracting party would then have a different national tariff schedule which it would apply to imports from all other countries, but negotiations in LAFTA rounds would start with offers and not, as in GATT, with requests.

A second track was the aim of drawing a common schedule to comply with the provision in Article XXIV of the General Agreement to free 'substantially all trade'. The common schedule would list the products on which all member countries agreed to eliminate duties, charges and other restrictions completely. The inclusion of products in this schedule would be final and the concessions granted irrevocable. Negotiations for the common schedule were to proceed in four three-year stages: during each three-year period 25 per cent of the products traded would be negotiated until 'substantially all' trade was covered.

The period up to 1973 was regarded as one of transition, during which the only reductions in effect would be those in national schedules. The common shedule would free subtantially all trade by 1973, but none of the reductions proposed would be put into effect until that date. The term 'substantially all' trade was not defined, but when LAFTA countries were asked to define the term by GATT in its review of the Treaty, they replied that it meant 'between 75% and the whole of the trade' (GATT, L/1311, 1960).

These two tracks revealed the traditional inter-industrial approach to trade upheld by Argentina, Brazil, Chile and Uruguay. A third track to trade liberalization was contemplated by Articles 16 and 17 on complementarity (intra-industrial) agreements, revealing ECLA's broader regional development visions. In line with ECLA's proposal, the purpose was to reduce duties and to agree on a division of labour within industrial sectors which could either be vertical or horizontal. Initially, the Treaty contemplated that such concessions for complementarity were to be granted on an MFN basis, but, in 1964, Resolution 99 (IV) waived MFN obligation and allowed concessions to be effective exclusively among the parties to the negotiation, with the proviso that 'adequate compensation' would be offered to those countries adversely affected.

The free-trade school carried considerable weight in drafting the provisions of the Treaty of Montevideo; in practice, however, an inward-looking trend prevailed throughout the region. More than a consequence of the theoretical debate, it responded to external constraints. Balance of payments weaknesses induced restrictions on trade and payments in hard currencies. Even though such measures were not always meant to be an integral part of import substitution or economic integration programmes, they none the less aimed to protect vulnerable trade and payments positions. This was even true for Venezuela, who enjoyed a special position of strength linked to her oil exports, and who remained aloof during LAFTA's formative years. By the end of 1960, when oil earnings began to dwindle and its balance of payments came under pressure, Venezuela resorted to currency devaluation, tariff increase and exchange and import controls (ECLA, *Economic Bulletin for Latin America*, Vol. 7, No. 1, p. 42; Dell, 1966, p. 47). In 1964 Venezuela announced its intention to join LAFTA.

Until 1968, regional exports grew more rapidly than world exports (de Vries, 1977). While this was happening, countries were not disinclined to offer each other incentives for stimulating such trade.

5.4 THE EXAMINATION OF THE TREATY OF MONTEVIDEO BY GATT

GATT appointed a Working Party to examine the compatibility of the Montevideo Treaty with the provisions of the General Agreement. An extensive questionnaire was prepared for the Latin American countries and the Working Party met twice, in June and November 1960, to study the legal implications of the replies. The Working Party was unable to reach a positive judgement. It was ambivalent as to whether the Treaty effectively guaranteed that a free-trade area would eventually be attained, since

there remain some questions of a legal and practical nature which it would be difficult to settle solely on the basis of the text of the Treaty and that these questions could be more fruitfully discussed in the light of the application of the Montevideo Treaty. For these reasons the Contracting Parties do not at this juncture find it appropriate to make recommendations to the parties to the Treaty [GATT, BISD, 9th S, p. 21.]

Doubtless, the method of annual negotiations on a product-by-product basis in addition to the leeway for withdrawal of concessions in national schedules was 'a far cry from the general unconditional and linear reductions to be found in the Treaty of Rome or the Stockholm Convention' (Lortie, 1975, p. 32). The cold reception was partly off-set by the consideration that such a decision should not prevent the entry into force of the Treaty.

Traces of open condemnation were removed by a statement made by Assistant-Secretary of GATT, Jean Royer, at ECLA's Conference in May 1961 in Santiago:

> We are satisfied with the entry into force of the Treaty of Montevideo which will have the double aim of providing a broader base for Latin American economic development without affecting its trade with industrial countries. The Contracting Parties are particularly grateful to the signatories of the Treaty of Montevideo for their efforts to adapt their association to the rules of GATT. [ECLA, Third Conference of the Committee on Trade, 8 May 1961, Press Release No. 3.]

Simultaneously with GATT's examination of the Treaty, Argentina began negotiations for accession to GATT. Argentina's Declaration of Provisional Accession (BISD, 9th S, p. 12) authorized the continuation of the preferential treatment granted to its neighbouring countries. These could not yet be covered by LAFTA, since the Treaty was to enter into force only the following year, followed immediately by the first round of negotiations held in Montevideo from 24 July to 12 August. By the time negotiations for Argentina's accession to GATT were completed, together with the conclusion of the Kennedy Round in 1967, the preferences had been accommodated into LAFTA. The government of Argentina then indicated 'that tariff preferences were no longer granted, the beneficiaries now being members of LAFTA'. (BISD, 15th S, p. 99.)

5.5 THREE DIFFERENCES WITH WESTERN EUROPEAN INTEGRATION

5.5.1 Intra-industrial and inter-industrial negotiations

In Western Europe, market integration was preceded by a significant level, not only of industrial trade, but of intra-industry trade also. Grubel and Lloyd calculated that before liberalization 53 per cent of total EEC trade was intra-industry. This indicates that already, before the formation of the EEC, there was no clearcut difference between 'export industries' and 'import-competing industries' (Grubel & Lloyd, 1975, pp. 135 ff), as conventional theories assume. Given this blurring of the functional features of the import-competing and the export-sector, liberalization was not only less costly but offered, moreover, an advantage to firms involved in this two-way trade and production. Two-way trade, having been an unplanned development of Western European industrial development was reinforced with trade liberalization. Grubel and Lloyd calculated that 71 per cent of the total growth in trade among EEC members between 1959 and 1967 took the form of an increase within industrial sectors.

In contrast, before the formation of LAFTA, industrial trade was insignificant and there was a clearcut differentiation between the predominantly primary export sector and the predominantly industrial import-competing one. With hindsight, it could be argued that ECLA's blueprints for industrial complementarity (as well as the equivalent 'integration industries' for the Central American Common Market), had they been implemented to the extent envisaged by ECLA, would have operated as planned intra-industry trade. Instead, complementarity agreements were relegated to a secondary role. LAFTA's initial negotiations concentrated on restoring the flow of traditional trade. Until 1964 the pace of product-by-product (inter-industry) concessions on national schedules was very active. Cuts were mainly made on primary products, consistent with the original aim of Argentina, Brazil, Chile and Uruguay.

As a result of the first three rounds of negotiations, trade among LAFTA countries recovered from the low point of US$ 299 million in 1961 to US$ 558 million in 1964. The share of such trade in their overall total likewise rose from 6 per cent in 1961 to 10 per cent in 1964 (Dell, 1966, p. 219). The pace of product-by-product negotiations stalled after 1964 for by then the 'easy' items of the region's traditional trade had run out and a new stage would have meant that countries would have to make room to accommodate imports. As from the third round of negotiations, members became more reluctant to offer concessions for their competitive industrial products which in most countries enjoyed high tariff protection (INTAL, 1968, p. 63). Moreover, negotiations for the common schedule which ought to have started by 1963 never got off the ground.

In theory the principle of reciprocity in tariff negotiations is designed to achieve a balanced expansion of trade and so to smooth resistance to tariff cuts since a concession granted will be matched by an equivalent concession on another product of export interest. Yet in inter-industry negotiations, for the businesses involved, this sort of reciprocity offers few incentives. If a tariff reduction on canned pineapples is exchanged for an equivalent concession (however defined) on timber products, it is most unlikely that firms and labour producing canned pineapples in the importing country can be encouraged by the increased export opportunities provided for timber products. The firms affected by tariff cutting will have a defensive attitude in such circumstances. Liberalization becomes politically costly, however rational it may be as an economic choice.

To counterbalance business resistance, and develop grassroots support for liberalization, beginning in 1963, the LAFTA Secretariat began to invite industrial firms to its headquarters in Montevideo to discuss trade opportunities in their respective sectors. Business participation was indeed enhanced by technocratic nudging: between seventeen and twenty such meetings took place every year though they did not always lead to significant progress in tariff cuts. Yet this mechanism for tariff cuts, at first regarded as heterodox and mainly as a mobilizing accessory, gradually began to gain in importance. By the time the pace of inter-industry negotiations had slackened, intra-industry tariff negotiations still retained some vitality. Tariff dismantling thus proceeded along two trails: the traditional inter-industrial one and the more heterodox intra-industrial course which led to a number of complementarity agreements. In the final shaping of these, the role of central economic planning was minimal, however, in comparison to what ECLA had originally advocated.

It was unsurprising—indeed natural—that within the private sector MNCs were initially most alert to the opportunities opened by intra-industry discussions. The presence in several member countries of branches of the same parent company gave such firms access to a unique regional vision. The minutes of the meetings held in Montevideo indicate that more than 50 per cent of the participants were representatives of MNCs; in sectors such as electrical and electronic products, office machines and chemicals and pharmaceuticals, foreign participation reached 80 per cent (INTAL, INV/12/dtl, 1968). The first sectoral agreement was signed between the governments of Argentina, Brazil, Chile and Uruguay in 1962 (GATT, L/1861) at the behest of IBM even before the periodical business meetings in Montevideo had got started. It was in effect an intra-firm arrangement aimed at vertical country specialization.

Although the intra-industry mechanism proved to be relatively more dynamic than the conventional inter-industry approach, the 3,500 concessions in complementarity agreements covered only 7 per cent of regional trade, compared to over 13,000 concessions on national schedules. These, despite their slack progress since the early stages, covered around 50 per cent of regional trade. The stumbling progress along the inter-industry track and the disappointing coverage of complementarity agreements is essentially due to the rival profile of LDCs' industrialization, their trade being still mainly a remnant of domestic production. Foreign markets are found if and when there is such a residue. In such circumstances trade does not grow in response

Table 5.2 Pace of concessions

Year	No. of concessions granted in national tariff schedules	No. of concessions granted by complementarity agreements
1961	4,268	—
1962	4,495	25[a]
1963	875	—
1964	306	51
1965	765	—
1966	432	20
1967	1,124[b]	491
1968	732	195
1969	242	114
1970	35	1,332
1971	52	150
1972	51	875
1973	34	—
1974	1	—
1975	21	93
1976	9	—
1977	10	219
1978	17	21
Total	13,469	3,576

[a] These are concessions agreed within the IBM intra-firm arrangement.
[b] The jump in 1967 is due to Venezuela's accession and its 'entry fee' of 517 concessions.
Source: Own elaboration from Consejo Argentino para las Relaciones Internacionales, 1979. Tables 11 and 12, pp. 46–7.

to foreign demand; it must find its own demand. Trade here is the means by which production in excess of a country's domestic absorption finds its way abroad.

In contrast, as outlined in Chapter 3, trade among developed countries was in general terms no longer following this pattern. It could advance smoothly because trade was growing by more than production. This implied that trade grew in response to demand, making developed economies more interdependent and less rivalrous. The competitive phase of their industrial development had led in its time to a scramble for raw materials and export outlets; it had been largely completed by the end of World War II. Nowadays, in technology-intensive sectors with oligopolistic features such as intra-industry trade and product differentiation, markets are found before production takes place.

Why it should be asked, did MNCs not make more use of the expanded regional market? It is frequently accepted that 'the international companies' concern is to achieve least cost production over the world' (Behrman, 1972, p. 81). Yet profits may and do in fact take precedence over efficiency; these may not only be derived from efficient production. With replicated investments spread throughout Latin America behind high national tariff barriers, international firms remained largely defensive of their import substitution pattern of investment. Although in theory international companies were expected to welcome a larger market in which to invest, in fact, if they had to face competition in their local market from outsiders, their past tariff-jumping investment would become less profitable. The above-cited study by Behrman, despite the dictum quoted, also reported that officials of nineteen MNCs, at a meeting nine years after LAFTA's formation, could not think of a single investment made by any private firm to serve a regionally integrated market.

All recognise that integration means rationalisation of the industry to a smaller number of companies. None of them can afford to initiate the suggestion for fear of being asked to drop out. ... All want the opportunities provided by a continuing presence; if they drop out their options for the future are narrowed significantly. [Behrman, 1972, p. 116.]

Only in isolated instances, such as IBM's initiative in the first complementarity agreement, were international investments planned to serve the regional market. IBM was then a new entrant to the market. For established companies, lower external tariff protection did not have the same positive repercussions. An UNCTAD study takes an example from the Andean Pact and traces the opposition of Chrysler to regional rationalization; the study concludes that 'the larger the volume of a company's pre-integration production, the stronger will be its aversion to integration' (UNCTAD, 1982, p. 7). Whereas for IBM trade would not displace production (it would in fact lead to new production), for old-established companies production would have to be trimmed to make room for imports from competing firms. In such circumstances trade was viewed with misgivings.

5.5.2 Payments

We noted in Chapter 3 that trade and capital flows have been intimately connected. Capital flows have largely served to finance trade. The problem of payments and the availability (or lack) of foreign exchange is of relevance to regional integration as much as it is to trade in general. The right to discriminate in trade under GATT's Article XXIV does not carry with it the right to discriminate in payments. A free-trade area only gives members the right to negotiate commercial concessions, not the right to negotiate financial arrangements to cover the flow of trade that might eventually be created. This is a function of the IMF.[8] Notwithstanding the IMF's recommendation, Western Europe set up the European Payments Union (EPU) in 1950 before the Treaty of Rome. The IMF also strongly opposed the creation of an automatic system of reciprocal credits for LAFTA.

Dell has pointed out that opposition to special payments arrangements for Latin America was based on the assumption that any such arrangements would involve the abandonment of financial discipline and responsibility (Dell, 1966, p. 163). A second reason advanced against following the EPU model is that while in Western Europe in the 1950s intra-regional trade accounted for 40 per cent of total trade, in Latin America the equivalent proportion was in the order of 10 per cent. Since intra-regional trade comprised such a small proportion of total trade, the orthodox view held that a special currency mechanism for intra-regional trade scarcely seemed to be warranted. In contrast, the less orthodox view held that it was imperative not merely to consolidate trade flows, as is the case with developed countries, but to create such trade flows (GATT, L/1861/Add.1, 1962, p. 5). An appropriate currency mechanism would help trade opportunities to develop.

However, Argentina, Chile and Brazil were not in a position to flout IMF views. The Paris Club was rescheduling their debt at that time and a condition of such rescheduling was that the country should undertake IMF-monitored stabilization programmes. To compensate for the lack of a payments system, the central banks relied on a network of bilateral credit agreements that failed to provide sufficient incentives.

The genesis of the controversy on trade and money, like the controversy on prices and markets, can be traced back to the debate between the economists of industrially advanced England and the Alexander Hamilton and Friedrich List schools. At the heart of the debate lies the role of money. Whereas the mercantilist concentrates on foreign exchange as the principal scarce resource to be economized, the free trader is concerned with the scarcity of real resources which need to be maximized via international specialization and the gains from trade. Money, to the free trader, is simply a lubricant (or Adam Smith's great wheel) that, through divisions of labour and commercial exchanges, makes savings in scarce real resources.

But the perception of foreign exchange scarcity in Latin America was not simply derived from a mercantilist stance on the role of money. Central to ECLA'S prescriptions was its theory of deteriorating terms of trade (Chapter 2). Moreover, the end of the Korean war revived a period in which the terms of trade of primary goods steadily declined. ECLA held that 'deterioration of the terms of trade [was] materially reducing the positive contribution of international financial resources' (Prebisch *et al.*, 1966, p. 286) to Latin American development. The gap between export earnings and import needs widened and the balance of payments came under pressure in one country after another. Most countries resorted to devaluations, import controls and payments restrictions in order to preserve their inadequate foreign exchange earnings for vital imports. ECLA furthermore had a pessimistic evaluation of the long-term trends of the primary commodities markets. Owing to severe oversupply Latin America could not rely on commodity exports for its development.

Inadequate reserves meant that full currency convertibility and financial orthodoxy, to conform strictly with multilateralism, could not be sustained. The Latin American countries were only able to maintain convertibility by applying very severe restrictions on trade and by resorting to heavy exchange surcharges and prior deposit systems. Under such conditions currency convertibility became little more than a formality: the form was there without substance. Trade and payments restrictions required to sustain convertibility are just as disruptive of the international division of labour as the maintenance of inconvertibility of currencies.

Moreover, little external finance to tide over the periods of balance of payments disequilibrium was available to LDCs in the 1960s. Capital flows were mostly in the form of official bilateral loans (which by and large tended to be tied), suppliers' credits (Griffith-Jones, 1983) and direct private investments. We have seen in Chapter 3 how the share of direct private investment going to LDCs declined sharply throughout the period. Also, direct investment is not alone in being tied to specific sectors or corporations; so also are suppliers' credits and most official loans. In balance of payments disequilibria, countries could apply to the IMF, whose assistance was subject to the adoption of onerous adjustment policies centred on the reduction of spending and on the increase in exportable surpluses through demand management and devaluation. Most governments approached it with hesitation.[9] But the 1970s brought a dramatically changed situation with the lending boom to LDCs. The reasons for this growth have been explained many times and in many ways; they need not be analysed here. Suffice it to note that one of the main reasons, though by no means the only one, was the sharp rise in the price of oil in 1973 and the concomitant financial surpluses in the hands of OPEC countries. Lacking sufficient capacity to absorb such funds and expertise in foreign financial markets, they deposited their surpluses with the transnational banks on a short-term basis in the Euromarket system. A feature of the Euromarket has been the freedom of banks from official controls; national monetary authorities did not intervene with their business decisions. This allowed the banks the operational flexibility to borrow short term from their depositors and lend long term to their borrowers. The initial clients of the Euromarket were in the developed countries, but as their demand for funds slackened by 1976, owing to the impact of the recession, banks were prompted to seek out new business. Countries that had previously been considered 'unacceptable' clients were offered tempting terms. Throughout the 1970s LDCs were consequently able to obtain finance for their balance of payments deficits without needing (as they had in the previous period) to undergo a dose of austerity. There is also evidence that this increased borrowing was used to boost foreign exchange reserves, either to replace the sharp falls of previous years or to obtain a larger cushion of reserves than the countries had previously had (Table 5.3).

International bank credits in Eurocurrencies (including bond operations) were estimated to have exceeded $111 billion in 1978, or almost four times the amount in 1973. Of this vast expansion Latin American countries received a substantial share. In 1973 they received 12 per cent of all such loans (or 41 per cent of the resources contracted by LDCs as a whole). In 1979 Latin American countries absorbed 23 per cent of all Euroloans, or 53 per cent of the total flows to LDCs (IDB, 1979, pp. 82 ff). Even more striking than Latin America's share in total lending was the growth in the net flow of external funds received. From 1961 to 1966 the level of external financing was relatively stable, at around $1.6 billion annually. This flow rose to $4.7 billion in 1972. From 1972 to 1979 there was a fivefold increase in value. This upward trend is evident not only from the increase in nominal value, a part of which merely reflects the devaluation of the dollar: in addition, the net flow of external financing received rose as a proportion of GNP from an average of 2 per cent in 1961–6 to 2.4 per cent in 1967–72, and to 4.4 per cent in 1973–8.

The increase in the overall volume of external capital inflows was due to the sharp rise in private financing. While official flows grew by a mere 38 per cent from $1,459 billion from 1973 to 1979, private credit in the form both of loans and of bond issues in Eurocurrency markets increased nearly fivefold. Foreign loans on that scale had seldom been available and thus the Latin American countries were able to accumulate monetary reserves in an unprecedented manner over this period (see Table 5.3). The changes in financial markets offered the Latin American countries a novel option in foreign economic policy. One factor which had inspired import substitution—the lack of foreign exchange—was removed. Although borrowing obviously entailed a heavy liability for future debt servicing, it created an immediate 'cushion' to sustain an increased flow of imports. Access to foreign credits on competitive terms allowed the economies to open up to international competition. The previous consensus on foreign exchange savings and import substitution gave way to an emphasis on freer import policies.

Advice from international institutions was again forthcoming, though this time the source was not ECLA. Anne O. Krueger's influential study for the National Bureau of Economic Research on trade liberalization in selected LDCs judged that:

> The lesson would appear to be that transition from exchange control to liberalisation can best be achieved by adopting a sliding peg at a realistic exchange rate and simultaneously *borrowing a quantity of foreign exchange*

Table 5.3 Gross official international monetary reserves of LAFTA countries, 1972–1979 (in $m at year end)

Country	1972	1973	1974	1975	1976	1977	1978	1979	1980	
Argentina	465.0	1,318.0	1,313.0	457.0	1,614.0	3,331.0	5,147.0	9,388.0[a]	9,139.0[a]	(July)
Bolivia	59.7	70.4	193.4	156.8	168.7	236.5	197.0	207.0	177.1[a]	(Sept)
Brazil	4,183.0	6,416.0	5,272.0	4,036.0	6,544.0	7,256.0	11,894.0	9,688.0	6,159.0[a]	(July)
Chile	148.3	179.7	101.8	110.7	461.5	484.1	1,148.8	2,377.9	3,820.9	(Sept)
Colombia	325.0	532.0	449.0	523.0	1,161.0	1,820.0	2,503.0	4,058.0	5,033.0	(Sept)
Ecuador	143.4	241.1	349.7	286.1	515.2	670.5	686.7	784.3	972.6[a]	(Sept)
Mexico	1,164.0	1,355.0	1,393.0	1,538.0	1,398.0	1,928.0	2,264.0	2,988.0	2,298.0[a]	(April)
Paraguay	31.5	57.1	87.2	115.1	157.6	268.1	449.2	613.5	739.7[a]	(Sept)
Peru	483.9	568.4	967.5	467.8	331.6	399.1	432.1	1,627.1	2,120.7	(July)
Uruguay	203.0	240.0	232.0	392.0	490.0	742.0	849.0	971.0	1,111.0	(July)
Venezuela	1,732.0	2,412.0	6,506.0	8,875.0	8,596.0	8,210.0	6,516.0	7,768.0	8,282.0	(Sept)

[a] Excludes gold.
Source: Interamerican Development Bank, *Annual Reports*, 1978 and 1980.

sufficient to permit an immediate liberalisation of imports (to the extent that the premium on import licenses disappears) *and to assure observers that the liberalisation will continue* ... One implication for this project is that providing such loans might have a high social product in terms of the allocation of world resources if the loans were utilised in conjunction with a consistent program to increase foreign exchange earnings and so sustain liberalisation. (Own emphasis.) (Krueger, 1978, pp. 240–1.]

The Inter-American Development Bank (IDB) also adjusted its philosophy. In a speech delivered in May 1979, the President of the IDB, Antonio Ortiz Mena, stated that an important priority of the Bank in the period was to support the attempts of the Latin American countries to improve their efficiency by opening their economies to the world market. The objective was 'to play a different role in the new structure of comparative advantages evolving worldwide ... to participate under improved conditions in this new international division of labour' (*Revista de Integración Latinoamericana*, 36, June 1979, p. 70). Thus, the ability to raise funds in the commercial market and the consequent inflow of financial resources provided the lubricant that had been lacking.[11] An increase in imports was encouraged in the belief that they would serve, *inter alia*, to modernize and increase the efficiency of industry. In Argentina and Chile, over and above the near elimination of protective barriers, an overvalued exchange rate, manipulated to bring down inflation (Fitzgerald, 1983; Díaz Alejandro, 1983), led to an import boom. Based on the conventional inter-industry interpretation of international trade, remedial measures were designed to improve 'efficiency' in what was thought to be a price-competitive world. Thus, any attraction that the regional market had to offer was lost from sight. Import substitution had not provided sufficient incentive for regional integration to be completed (after the fashion of the EEC). What failed to materialize was expanded intra-industry trade, or in its absence, the planning of import substitution at a regional level as envisaged by ECLA. But import substitution at the country level had nevertheless been a (perhaps the prime) motivator of regional trade. Latin American integration was thus locked into a vicious circle in which the import substitution pattern of production hindered the further growth of trade; yet, at the same time, what trade there was, was motivated by import substitution. The dependence of existing trade on import substitution will be seen more clearly in the following section.

5.5.3 Margins of preference

Countries can change their MFN tariff levels (both upwards and downwards if they are unbound, only downwards if bound in GATT), so the lack of a common external tariff in LAFTA implied that margins of preference could fluctuate, affecting regional trade conditions. Fluctuations entail a risk since profitability may be reduced and so confidence in the regional market can not develop. Nevertheless, the margins of preference seem to have been a factor in encouraging what trade there was.

Apart from oil, a large proportion of intra-LAFTA trade has effectively been conducted under preferential concessions. In nominal terms, this was fluctuated from a record high of 90 per cent in 1964 to 53 per cent in 1977. When disaggregated into pairs of countries, these figures become even more revealing, as can be inferred from Table 5.4. Ninety-six per cent of Mexico's exports to Argentina in 1976 were covered by LAFTA concessions. So were 64 per cent of its exports to Chile. In the case of Colombia the proportion of LAFTA-concession-covered exports to Argentina and Chile was 100 and 61 per cent respectively. Similarly, all Ecuadorian exports to Argentina were covered by concessions.

The final blow to LAFTA came, just as twenty years earlier its impetus had come, from the southernmost countries. The coup in Chile in 1973 and that in Argentina in 1976 established autocratic regimes with neo-classical economic philosophies. With the cushion provided by foreign borrowing, radical trade liberalization programmes were adopted. Chile enforced a maximum tariff of 10 per cent (similar to the average EEC Common External Tariff), Argentina intended to have a maximum tariff of 25 per cent by 1984. Uruguay followed suit with a plan to achieve a maximum tariff of 35 per cent.[12] Such extreme liberalization could not but have an impact on their LAFTA partners. The reason for this lies essentially in the fact that across-the-board tariff cuts dealt a blow to the margin of preference that LAFTA members had been granting each other so that an important incentive to buy in LAFTA was removed. In effect, if the margin of preference is reduced to negligible levels, its impact on the final price of goods is also negligible. With no exchange restrictions and low tariff levels, new business opportunities arise from trade with third countries as factors such as shipping costs, export credits and after-sales service come into play.

By 1978 Argentina had either reduced or eliminated the margin of preference on 94 per cent of the concessions that had previously benefited LAFTA members. Ninety-five per cent of Chilean concessions underwent a similar process (Consejo Argentino para las Relaciones Internacionales, 1979, p. 57). As these countries reduced or suppressed regional preferences, the remaining members of the association were inclined to reciprocate in self-defence. Without a margin of preference for their own exports, it was no longer in their interest to maintain a unilateral margin of preference for their imports from these countries. Countries seek to secure a balance between imports and exports that are traded under preferential arrangements in order to avoid either a deterioration in their own terms of trade or subsidizing the exports of their trading partners without receiving reciprocal treatment. Thus,

Table 5.4 Percentage of bilateral imports covered by LACTA concessions, 1976 (c.i.f. current prices)

Importer	Exporter											
	Argentina	Bolivia	Brazil	Colombia	Chile	Ecuador	Mexico	Paraguay	Peru	Uruguay	Venezuela	LAFTA
Argentina	—	11.8	56.2	99.9	74.5	99.9	96.0	92.4	65.5	11.1	18.8	54.5
Bolivia[a]	7.0	—	2.0	7.9	2.0	0.4	10.1	2.1	13.8	0.3	2.1	5.8
Brazil	94.1	44.9	—	55.1	98.1	99.8	89.2	98.9	44.2	85.9	1.2	82.4
Colombia	41.2	1.9	43.1	—	67.2	26.9	62.5	93.3	73.4	93.5	32.0	47.2
Chile[b]	37.4	3.4	38.0	61.3	—	12.5	64.0	65.2	51.3	3.5	3.6	33.9
Ecuador	12.6	—	12.5	19.3	47.9	—	34.5	91.0	19.8	6.5	0.9	24.1
Mexico[c]	13.8	1.2	88.2	85.6	77.7	53.7	—	72.7	83.9	33.7	0.6	42.0
Paraguay	12.2	—	16.2	29.5	77.4	70.0	51.5	—	—	11.8	0.6	14.5
Peru	17.6	—	8.7	4.9	3.3	—	28.7	74.2	—	34.1	5.3	6.1
Uruguay	12.5	—	16.7	12.0	16.8	—	22.8	29.8	37.1	—	0.1	14.2
Venezuela	7.0	—	12.6	3.3	7.0	2.4	12.5	32.8	3.3	0.2	—	8.9
Total	48.7	12.9	43.1	24.3	73.2	12.3	69.4	81.5	46.6	54.9	6.8	44.4

[a] Figures for 1972.
[b] Figures for 1974.
[c] Figures for 1975.

Source: Consejo Argentino de Relaciones Internacionales, La Argentina y el Proceso de Reestructuración de la ALALC (1980), p. 53.

the arduously negotiated LAFTA edifice, where all members applied high import duties to outsiders, stood on shaky ground. Most countries became reluctant to maintain regional multilateral concessions to countries with dissimilar economic policies. Some of the Andean Pact countries, Venezuela, Ecuador and Colombia, still favouring higher levels of tariff protection, were keen to withdraw concessions *vis-à-vis* the more efficiency-conscious countries. Peru and Bolivia, the other Andean countries,[13] were more ambiguous until 1980, when Peru also announced a reduction in import duties and Bolivia's economic policy fluctuated with the string of coups that took place at the time.

Although LAFTA had presided over a period in which an increase in regional trade had occurred, by 1980 it offered no further possibilities for advance along the same roads. Its obsolescence was formally acknowledged in August 1980 when agreement was reached on a reform, responding to the tension provoked by incompatible economic policies. The treaty launching the new Latin American Integration Association (LAIA) followed very closely the Argentinian blueprint for reform.[14] Chilean backing for the proposal was also important (*Revista de Integración Latinoamericana*, No. 44, May 1980).

5.6 GATT'S EVOLVING APPROACH TO REGIONAL ARRANGEMENTS

GATT had been specifically designed to arrest and reverse the spread of preferential trade agreements that had characterized the inter-war period. The underlying principle of Article XXIV is that a free trade area or a customs union, in contrast to a preferential area, must not only be a move toward freer regional trade but, over and above that, a first step towards freer global trade. Article XXIV views free-trade areas or customs union as initiating a movement towards freer trade whenever internal tariffs are completely eliminated on 'substantially all trade'. Yet 'the dismaying experience of the GATT has been that with one possible exception (the UK–Ireland Free Trade Area) no customs union or free trade area agreement . . . presented for review has complied with Article XXIV' (Dam, 1970, p. 275).

Although GATT was unsuccessful in forcing regional initiatives to conform precisely with the mould of Article XXIV, it was able to exercise leverage, when assisted, as in the case of LAFTA's inception, by a special set of circumstances, namely the divergence of views among the participant governments and the inclination of some of them to adhere to the multilateral framework as a gesture of goodwill to their creditors.[15] Where the regional initiative could muster greater bargaining power there was little GATT could do to enforce the rule of law. Realistically, Patterson judges that if an attempt had been made to force the European initiative and, in particular, its association agreements with overseas territories, to conform with the rules of Article

XXIV, 'the GATT itself probably would have been destroyed' (Patterson, 1966, p. 263).

In the wake of the adoption of Part IV (and the generally more lenient attitude regarding the commercial policies of LDCs in so far as they were not blatantly detrimental to the interests of developed countries), India, the United Arab Republic and Yugoslavia signed a Trade Expansion and Economic Co-operation Agreement in December 1967. As active participants in the Non-Aligned Movement and the Group of 77, the governments concerned took a more reformist attitude towards GATT. The treaty contemplated the reduction of MFN rates on an initial seventy-seven items, a further fifty-seven were added in a second stage and, lastly, another twenty-seven. The treaty was 'clearly outside the scope of Article XXIV . . . a purely preferential arrangement with no intention whatever of leading to a customs union or a free trade area in the long run' (Huber, 1981, p. 293), but there was no outright condemnation of the initiative in GATT. A similar reception was given to the Agreement of Bangkok in 1975 between India, Bangladesh, Laos, Philippines, South Korea, Sri Lanka and Thailand, 'during the examination of which the parties to the agreement did not even pretend that it constituted a customs union or a free trade area' (Huber, 1981, p. 286).

In 1977 Indonesia, Malaysia, Philippines, Singapore and Thailand formed the Association of East Asian Nations (ASEAN) and granted each other mutual preferences on selected products. It is noteworthy that this agreement took up the Latin American concept of 'complementarity agreements' for the eventual specialization of countries within industrial sectors.

Thus, by the time of the Tokyo Round, Article XXIV was honoured more in the breach than in the observance. The legal recognition that was lacking was finally granted with the so-called Enabling Clause (GATT, 1979, p. 149), which, as noted in Chapter 2, allowed LDCs to grant each other straightforward tariff preferences. Interested LDCs were then given the green light to put into motion a Global System of Tariff Preferences amongst them.

5.7 LAFTA'S SUCCESSOR: THE LATIN AMERICAN INTEGRATION ASSOCIATION

The Latin American Integration Association (LAIA) constitutes a further break with Article XXIV and previous regional integration formulae. Not only is it an outright preferential scheme, as are the others just mentioned; it also innovates by removing the obligation on participants to accord each other MFN treatment. One of the criticisms levelled at LAFTA had been that its MFN rule inhibited interested countries from seeking closer economic ties as tariff reductions had to be generalized to all members, and consequently the lowest common denominator prevailed (Consejo Argentino para las Relaciones Internacionales, 1979). LAIA allows members to grant each other bilateral concessions that need not automatically be extended to other member countries. Bilateral agreements of this sort are none the less left open for the accession of other countries with the intention that they should become progressively multilateralized. Newcomers, however, are required to enter into a new round of negotiations and offer concessions of their own to benefit from the existing ones. At least in its initial stages, then, LAIA is an umbrella for a host of bilateral preferential deals.

While LAFTA has endeavoured to 'promote progressively closer coordination of the corresponding industrialisation policies' (Article 16), by contrast LAIA will aim to 'facilitate the access of products to the world market' (Article 11). The report prepared by the Consejo Argentino para las Relaciones Internacionales considered that this was to be achieved by the new role to be played by regional preferences.[16] These would only be justified as temporary for as long as they contributed to an increase in the efficiency of production. The economic cost of discriminating against lower-cost third countries should only be borne with a view to enhancing productive capacity to reduce inefficiency, and as a first step leading to a situation in which competitiveness without a margin of preference was possible. Preferences should gradually be replaced by efficiency, at which stage exports to world markets should become feasible.

That Argentina was the most interested party in changing the rules under which she carried out her commercial transactions with the region can be explained if, instead of looking at her trade balances with LAFTA (which except for 1975 had been constantly positive), the share of trade under concessions is taken into account. Less than half of her exports were actually covered by concessions. As can be inferred from reading Table 5.4, in 1976 Argentina was granting preferential treatment to almost all her imports from Colombia, Ecuador, Mexico and Paraguay while only 41 per cent of her exports to Colombia, 13 per cent of those to Ecuador, 14 per cent to Mexico and 12 per cent to Paraguay were benefitting from reciprocal treatment. Similar disparities are evident in the trade with Chile and Peru. Brazil was the only country that purchased from Argentina more than it sold in the Argentine market under preferential arrangements. Thus, despite the positive balance of trade, the Argentine Government held that the country was not benefiting from regional preferences negotiated under LAFTA as much as its trading partners were. Argentine policy-makers argued that the country was subsidizing their exports without any evident quid pro quo. This hidden subsidy of other countries' exports was of special concern to an economic team that was not even inclined to subsidize its own domestic producers to aid them in foreign trade.[17]

Moreover, from Argentina's point of view, ending the MFN obligation to automatically extend all tariff concessions would avoid the repetition of the

LAFTA experience in which the asymmetry of preferential trade worked against her. If a third party becomes interested in joining a tariff agreement signed by two other countries, it can no longer hope to be a 'free rider'; it will now have to offer a similar concession by way of 'entry free'. In other words, this reform in the procedure for tariff reductions would enable countries to closely scrutinize the balance of their preferential imports and exports. Reciprocal treatment could be monitored at a country-to-country level, aided by the resolution to renegotiate existing preferences—the so-called 'historical patrimony' of LAFTA.

As MFN obligation was withdrawn, the Argentine sponsors of LAIA envisaged that closer economic cooperation among countries with harmonious structures and economic policies would be rendered possible. Such cooperation, they hoped, would take the form of an economic community among countries showing 'an ample base of shared values and interests' (Consejo Argentino para las Relaciones Internacionales, 1979, p. 140).

What was the impact of the change in policy instruments and the shift to bilateralism? The weight of these factors taken in isolation will be difficult to assess. Barely two years after the LAIA treaty had been signed, the region's debt crisis erupted. By mid-1982 hostile conditions in the world economy, falling earnings from commodity exports, industrial protection in international markets, world recession and the steep rise in real interest rates had led to a revival of the foreign exchange shortage that had characterized Latin America until the 1970s. Total imports had of necessity to be curtailed drastically as one country after the other faced severe balance of payments pressures. One after the other, hard-pressed governments were led to encourage domestic production of goods that had previously been imported. Regional exports shrank abruptly with the share of regional exports in total exports declining from 14 per cent in 1980 to 9 per cent in 1983, a share that was equivalent to that of 1960 when LAFTA was first launched. Although, in absolute terms, intra-regional trade shrank dramatically as the countries strove to secure trade surpluses to service their debts, in relative terms regional trade did not suffer as much as trade with third countries. Imports from LAIA did not fall as steeply as imports from the rest of the world (INTAL, International Trade Series, 1985), suggesting that regional imports may withstand the adverse impact of external recessions relatively better. Whereas, as in 1980, regional imports were 12.5 per cent of total imports, in 1983 they rose to 15.4 per cent. If oil is excluded, the share remains constant, just as it does if manufactured goods are taken on their own. This trend has been exceptionally marked in the case of Argentina where LAIA imports rose from 20 per cent in 1981 to 32 per cent in 1983. In a move to enhance exports, to meet their import needs and to overcome some of their financial shortages, Argentina and Brazil reached a trade accord in 1986 which set up a bilateral credits and payments system and aimed to promote intra-industrial specialization in the capital goods sector. This sector was selected not only owing to its potential for development; it is also an area in which some intra-industrial specialization is already manifest with Brazil showing an advantage in mass-market, serially produced machines and Argentina in high unit value, specialized products. The accord has raised high expectations, but doubtless, it marks a new stage in the too often frustrated attempts of LDCs to meet the challenge of economic progress through cooperation. The most innovative aspect of the initiative is that it aims to grant national treatment to a list of goods which will be exchanged at a zero tariff level; in addition equivalent tariffs will be applied to products from third countries.

Once again, regional trade will seemingly be used to compensate for the decline in exports to the world and the flow of hard currencies. Soft currency trade seems to be a second-best option that receives greater attention when conditions in international markets are hostile. The growth of LAFTA exports lagged behind the growth of exports to industrial countries when markets were buoyant. But in the recession of 1974–5, regional exports suffered declines that were less steep than exports to the rest of the world (de Vries, 1977). The pull of regional trade appears to follow fluctuations in external environment and serves as a buffer. While regional exports do not grow as fast as world exports, regional imports do not fall as steeply as imports from the rest of the world. Free trade-minded civil servants exerted significant influence in shaping both the LAFTA and LAIA treaties, yet the fate of regional trade seems to be affected more by these oscillations in the external environment than economic doctrines or legal documents.

5.8 CONCLUSIONS

This chapter has reviewed how GATT's rules on economic integration were adapted and applied in LAFTA and has shown that world market conditions played a greater role than the selection of policy instruments in the evolution of regional trade. In contrast to what was happening among developed countries and what was reflected in GATTs rounds of liberalization, no major local industrial interests supported trade liberalization. Both national and international firms were primarily interested in domestic markets, only secondarily in foreign markets and then only in exports, not in imports. In this they were aided by the import substitution policies of governments, each competing against the others to promote national industrial development. With the exception of a few MNCs, firms with an interest in exports were not simultaneously geared to take compensating imports, nor were governments keen on inducing them to do so.

Despite these caveats, regional margins of preference seemed to have played a role in stimulating trade, mainly along inter-industry lines, although it is difficult to judge how big a role and whether preferences were cause or consequence of trade expansion. All we can say is that the erosion of the margin of preference in the 1970s was coupled with a decreasing interest in the regional market.

It seems that Latin American countries will turn to each other when they turn inwards and this happens when unfavourable market conditions induce them to do so. For Latin America the 1930s was a case in point when, with their trade and financial links severed, a host of bilateral trade and exchange agreements grew up. LAFTA also arose at a time when Latin America's external export markets were generally soft and financial flows were insufficient to cover the gap. With the debt crisis, a similar set of circumstances seems to have arisen with a vengeance. When outward-looking policies prevail, the pull of the world market is stronger than that of the regional market. This is one reason why regional integration advanced in Latin America, albeit patchily, more than in other areas of the less developed world. In the newly industrializing ASEAN countries, where industrialization has been more outward- than inward-looking, industrial trade within ASEAN is second in importance to trade with the world market.

In Latin America inward-looking policies have been largely impelled by the shrinkage or the inadequacy of credit flows. One of the points made in this chapter is that money and trade cannot be understood in isolation. With inadequate purchasing power under the Bretton Woods financial system, freer trade with the world market was handicapped.[18] With the expansion of international bank lending during the 1970s, the pull of the world market gathered strength and inward-looking policies, both at a national and a regional level, lost their relative attraction.

When compared with trade among developed countries, regional trade in Latin America has another factor working against it. As described in Chapter 3, LDCs are not full participants in either oligopolized markets or in intra-industry trade. Their exports still mainly compete on price grounds, not having fully advanced to the kind of product differentiation that is so prevalent in developed countries. In such circumstances, exports do not grow in response to demand; they must find their own demand abroad and will tend to displace production at the import end. In South–South trade there is little intra-industrial specialization, which inhibits further trade expansion and little industrial trade occurs because of lack of specialization.

Two kinds of remedial measures were attempted to overcome this deadlock. One was based on intra-trade theory (perhaps more implicitly than explicitly), the other on inter-trade theory. The first of these was the creation of the Andean Pact in 1969, as a subgrouping in LAFTA. By co-ordinating industrial policies and their treatment with foreign investment, the Andean countries tried to go beyond the merely commercial aspects of trade to draw a link between trade and production. Implicitly, the Andean Pact acknowledged that trade among developed countries and, in particular in the EEC, had expanded vigorously, not simply as a result of tariff reductions. Other factors were at work supporting a vigorous trade sector (Chapter 3) and these allowed tariff reductions to be staged with relative ease. The Andean Pact (and LAFTA's complementarity agreements) tried to do by planning what in developing countries had to a large extent been unplanned. The policy was ahead of its time; it would have forced particular firms and countries to cut production.

The other set of remedial measures spearheaded by Argentina and Chile in the late 1970s was based on inter-trade assumptions. The lack of export growth was attributed to inefficiency and excessive protectionism. It is not suggested that industrial production should dismiss considerations of efficiency; but the prescription was based on a faulty picture of world trade which assumed it to be mainly a price-sensitive, price-competitive world.

LAFTA's first watershed was certainly the creation of the Andean Pact. But to a great extent the Andean–non-Andean split, until the import-freeing wave of the 1970s, was one of national versus regional industrial integration. Up to that point there had been a consensus on a policy of protection for industrial development with differences limited to whether it should be regional or national. When the liberalizing drive took off the issue became one of regional integration versus world market integration. The final blow to LAFTA came with the erosion of all traces of positive discrimination for regional trade flows.

The obvious judgement to be made on LAFTA is simply that it failed; yet before accepting this view out of hand it is well to recall the limited original objective of Argentina, Uruguay, Chile and Brazil. But there was more to it than that: the regional market contributed to the diversification of exports and offered the opportunity of learning by doing. Lastly, although the regional market remained vulnerable to externally sparked changes, it is possible that it may operate as a safety net in times of difficulty in world markets. A lesson that LAFTA has left for the future of the Global System of Tariff Preferences among LDCs is that it will not go far if it does not work in tandem with a payments and credits arrangement. 'Everything is difficult for the under-developed countries, not least their mutual cooperation' (Myrdal, 1956, p. 266).

NOTES

1. There has been only modest progress since the conclusion of the Tokyo Round to set up a Global System of Trade Preferences among LDCs.
2. See Chapter 2.
3. The margin of preference is the difference between the duty applied to imports from these neighbouring countries and imports from third countries.

4. See Chapter 2 for the two different stages that Prebisch envisaged for exports of LDCs.

5. FitzGerald (1983) refers to the role played by economic theory as an organizing ideology for state bureaucrats, both of the free trade and the structuralist variety.

6. See Chapter 4 for the implications of the notion of 'market disruption'.

7. Non-reciprocal concessions in LAFTA suffered a similar fate to the Generalized System of Preferences. Very few have been put to much use and those of any value have been fewer. As with GSP, 'preferential treatment . . . was left to a continuous process of negotiations, in which, of course, the weaker parties were permanently at a disadvantage' (Salgado, 1979, p. 126).

8. General Agreement, Article XV, paragraph 2, 'in all cases in which the Contracting Parties are called upon to consider or deal with problems concerning monetary reserves, balance of payments or foreign exchange arrangements they shall consult fully with the IMF'. GATT's examination of the Treaty of Montevideo dealt with LAFTA's intentions on the matter, and the governments duly declared that they did not intend to give any preferential treatment in respect of credits with LAFTA (Question 24, GATT, L/1311, November 1960).

9. Thorp and Whitehead have suggested that 'the practice of attaching economic policy conditions to the provision of Fund resources was gradually developed during the 1950s, mainly using Latin American economies as the testing ground for these techniques.' (Thorp & Whitehead, 1979, p.3).

10. This extensive study was influential in World Bank/IMF circles from the early 1970s when initial conclusions were first made public. See, for example, papers delivered to the Seminar on Export Promotion Policies held in Santiago in November 1976.

11. Another feature of this period was the export credit race among OECD countries that enabled exporters to offer goods on concessional terms to foreign clients, terms that regional governments could not easily match.

12. The only sector that was spared from the drastic removal of protection was the car industry, with which a gradual reorganization programme was agreed. Local manufacturers of audio equipment, for instance, turned to importing similar goods to those they had previously produced. They were not unique. Officials at UNCTAD's division for assistance on the Generalized System of Preferences noted that, ever since the new economic policies were launched in Chile and Argentina, they had ceased to receive requests for assistance from local companies that had previously been active beneficiaries of the system. (Information supplied in a private communication.)

13. Chile, a founding member of the Andean Pact, had withdrawn from it when Pinochet came to power.

14. The Argentine proposal was reproduced in *Revista de Integración Latinoamericana*, 36, June 1979, pp. 78–81.

15. Argentina's immediate acceptance of the Tokyo Round agreements in April 1979, as soon as the document was open for signing, while the rest of the LDCs, including the Latin American countries, had proposed boycotting the affair, suggests a reptition of similar circumstances. The government was applying for fresh loans from the private banks at the time and the Minister for the Economy stopped in Geneva, before starting his fund-raising itinerary to show the resoluteness of his trade liberalization programme.

16. The Consejo Argentino para las Relaciones Internacionales is not an official government body but a grouping of ex-foreign affairs ministers with considerable influence in policy formulation. The report on the restructuring of LAFTA was

commissioned to three influential free traders, among whom were Roberto Alemann (Minister for the Economy in 1960 at the time of LAFTA's formation and then again under President Galtieri) and Jorge Wehbe (Minister in 1962 and again under President Bignone).

17. At UNCTAD V, the Argentine Under-Secretary for Trade and International Economic Negotiations declared that LDCs must co-operate to remove restrictions on international trade (Argentine Republic, *Economic Information on Argentina*, May 1979, p. 11.) At home he warned exporters not to expect subsidies, saying that these do not increase competitiveness, which can only be achieved by 'economic reform' (*El Cronista Comercial*, 17 November 1980).

18. This underlay Keynes's proposal for an International Clearing Union. If trade was to be free, believed Keynes, it was imperative to ensure that there would be no lack of international money to finance it and that the distribution of such money should be balanced.

6 The lessons of experience: looking back before looking ahead

Economic institutions are created from the currently accepted economic theories. At the time of GATT's foundation, trade and capital theory paralleled each other with the premiss that trade in goods was at least a partial substitute for the movement of factors. Accordingly, the Bretton Woods planners envisaged separate institutions for the management of trade and capital flows: the World Bank, originally known as the International Bank for Reconstruction and Development, to assist with capital flows, and the International Trade Organization (eventually the GATT) to deal with trade. A third institution, the International Monetary Fund, was set up to deal with problems of current account.

Trade theory at the time was largely normative theory. It aimed to demonstrate how trade and specialization could improve world and national welfare. GATT was stamped with this mark of origin despite a concession to pragmatism acknowledging the need to protect full employment. While the movement of capital was to be largely free, the movement of labour was not.

The GATT's founding philosophy was based on two key principles, one political—the sovereign equality of states—the other economic—factor proportions and comparative costs theory. With the competitive model of world trade in mind, tariffs were preferred over any other form of protection because they were seen as allowing the 'price mechanism' to operate. According to this image of international trade, countries would gradually specialize in those goods which they could produce relatively more efficiently. The attraction that the GATT procedure seemed to offer was that the process would be one of gradual accommodation. Moreover, should the process of adjustment prove too rapid or too disruptive, Article XIX offered the possibility of withdrawing and renegotiating a bound concession.

The GATT philosophy, however, has turned out to be only in tenuous relationship with the realities of world trade. World trade diverged from the two founding principles of the GATT almost from the start as capital mobility blurred national frontiers and made price competition recede into the background. Paradoxically, this was precisely the source of the GATT's success. To put it crudely, the GATT was successful because its two key principles had in practice ceased to be fully applicable. Tariff reductions were achieved and trade was liberalized, but it grew for reasons other than the price competition between countries or firms. The transformation of modern industrial activities meant that old-style price competition was relegated to a secondary role while other forms of competition, on the grounds of quality, model and innovation came to the fore. The new forms of competition were made possible by the increasing technological component in industry. Technology, being an ownership-specific advantage, allows firms to move away from being price-takers to being price-setters, at least for the period of time until the knowledge becomes diffused. Yet the full trade implications of these changes were not realized and old attitudes lingered on, giving way only gradually.

LDCs challenged the principles of international specialization but their responses were largely based on assumptions similar to those they were trying to challenge. They too drew a picture of the world economy largely centred on the assumption that factors were immobile and that trade relations were based on the relative ability to compete on price.

The initial negotiating stance of the LDCs in the 1950s and 1960s aimed at expanding their rights to deviate from the general rules of the GATT. The thrust of their action took two routes: one dealing with their exports, the other with their imports. As regards their exports, they lobbied for the right to extend tariff preferences to each other and for access to developed countries' markets; they also asked to be released from the obligations to grant reciprocity in tariff negotiations. With respect to imports, they demanded greater flexibility to protect their internal markets for their infant industries under Article XVIII.

The infant industry argument for protection is no alien to liberal economic theory, having been enshrined by J. S. Mill in his *Principles of Political Economy*. GATT's Article XVIII clearly reflects the infant industry line of argument; implicitly the demand for tariff preferences is also an infant industry approach in which the concern with the domestic market is replaced by the concern for external markets. The argument was put that, where exports of manufactured goods were concerned, LDCs met on the world market well-established, highly productive competitors whom in most branches they could not undersell. They maintained that, when the advanced countries industrialized, they had been in the privileged position of being surrounded by the untilled markets of underdeveloped countries which they could use as outlets for their manufactured production and thereby achieve economies of scale. This was one of the invaluable advantages of being ahead of the rest. Latecomers were unable to follow the same road. Yet, in attempting to reach a more balanced, integrated economy, LDCs needed to build up their industries and to diversify their exports. To counterbalance their handicap, they needed preferential treatment in the markets of the advanced countries.[1]

Although at the time these issues seemed to be serious bones of contention, in retrospect the demands of LDCs were accommodated with relative ease.

The most contentious issue was that of preferences because of the strong opposition of the United States. But here the LDCs had an advantageous bargaining position because of the differing views among the potential donors of preferences. The European countries had a pre-Bretton Woods tradition of preferential treatment for their colonial territories and the Treaty of Rome proposed to revive it.

Both kinds of demand, the protection of domestic markets and preferential tariff treatment in external markets, were based on the rationale that what was required was a helping hand to gradually actualize potential comparative advantage. With respect to the GATT, all that was needed was a release for LDCs from their fully-fledged obligations, in order to increase their room to manœuvre within the system. The reform took a negative approach by presenting the LDCs as a special case in need of exceptional treatment. What was required was agreement to remove LDCs from so-called 'normal' procedures in order to reduce the weight of GATT rules. In this way the GATT would become compatible with LDCs' handicaps and would allow a favourable climate of gestation for their incipient industrialization.

Despite amendments, frictions persisted and LDCs remained inadequately integrated. They remained somewhat restricted in their export outlets and many were driven to rely on domestic growth. One explanation ventured for the bias in the GATT has very often been that LDCs lacked sufficient bargaining power. Certainly bargaining power between LDCs and developed countries is asymmetrical. This is obvious. Much of the argument of the preceding chapters has been concerned with going beyond this statement. An explanation narrowly based on bargaining power fails to account for the different treatment of products originating in the same countries, i.e. why exports of steel encounter obstacles and why electrical machinery does not, why T-shirts are restricted and car parts are not. Moreover, when bargaining power was less asymmetrical, as among the member countries of LAFTA, trade expansion encountered equally significant obstacles.

Reasons must be found in the economic trends that international trade policy could not but follow. Chapter 3 identified four central trends that could go a long way towards explaining the successes and failures of GATT. Trade was concentrated among countries that were also drawn together by capital flows. Capital and trade have been intimately connected. Exports of capital have not replaced exports of goods; they have gone hand in hand. The two great eras of capital exports (1880–1913 and the contemporary period, beginning with the end of World War II) were also periods which saw the greatest growth in world trade.

Since the end of the War, developed countries have invested more in each other's markets and have traded more with each other than they have with LDCs. This points to a second feature of post-war trade expansion. Trade has been concentrated among countries not characterized by extreme disparities

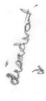

in their factor endowments and cost structure. Firms and countries carved market shares by differentials, not of price, but of qualities or features of the products sold. Adjustment to trade did not entail relocation of industrial sectors as had been anticipated, but accommodation within industries. Intra-industry trade meant that trade became bilaterally balanced, that is, there was a narrowing of the balance (exports minus imports) in each product relative to the value of total trade (exports plus imports) in that product. With intra-industrial specialization, some of the most painful features of adjustment to changing patterns of trade were overcome. Instead of contraction of production and emigration of industries to other countries, change could be managed within the firm or at least the industry. None of the countries participating in intra-industrial specialization had to relinquish production or let control of production go out of their hands.

Intra-industrial specialization was made possible by a third trend— the increasingly oligopolistic structure of the market. Firms became conglomerates or multi-product enterprises and expanded worldwide; those engaged in international trade and investment did not operate under conditions of atomistic competition. As production became concentrated, a degree of concertation among firms emerged. Some of the most ruthless aspects of competition were ironed out; some of the grounds for international economic friction among the countries so linked were to that extent eroded.

Lastly, as firms became multinational, they could engage in intra-firm trade, thereby drawing the benefits that could be derived from international specialization into their control. International specialization did not push them out of business but became part of their business as gains were internalized. In sectors and among countries where these transformations did not occur, trade encountered numerous obstacles. It was an uphill struggle. In sum, success in trade liberalization and expansion came not through price competition but precisely in sectors and among countries where firms ceased to be price-takers and where other forms of competition prevailed over the old-style competition.

In price competition, goods respond to market forces; they are sold to and from stock at a market-determined price. The exporters will add to the volume of goods available in the importing country. They can influence the price relationship prevailing in the importing country's market; moreover, under free-trade conditions they can absorb more than just a part of the market. In oligopolistic competition, production and marketing take place simultaneously: production is geared to pre-determined uses and users. The exporters will increase the selection of goods available in the importing country; its price relationships are respected and a part of the market only can be absorbed. It was easier to remove tariffs when production had been organized to take place simultaneously with marketing. This could be done more successfully in countries and in sectors where production had become concentrated than when it remained unconcentrated and price-competitive. Success in organizing production and gearing it to specific uses and users was translated into harmonious trade liberalization. Where production took place under oligopolistic conditions, international trade ceased to be about prices or, more precisely, it was only to a limited extent about prices. First and foremost, firms competed on quality and model grounds with differentiated products and rapid innovation in such products. When price rules prevailed, the response was to counter them with trade regulations so that market shares between domestic and foreign suppliers were not upset, irrespective of price competition. 'Orderly marketing arrangements' or 'voluntary' export restraints were sought to bring to the sector the order that was found wanting at the time of trading.[2] In coming GATT rounds oligopolistic competition will tend to be reflected in the insistence by developed countries on strict regulations to protect patents, trademarks, and intellectual property rights.

Japan was the first so-called 'newly industrializing country' to feel the brunt of protectionist pressures and at the same time to grasp the tacit new rules. Japan started by exporting standardized, labour-intensive goods at low prices; when friction was encountered, it moved away from these goods. By the mid-1970s, Japanese textiles had ceased to be a threat to the developed importing countries. Although frictions persisted in steel, cars, videos and a number of other products, the Japanese tended to be amenable when requested either to restrict the volume of their exports or to raise their export prices. This, in fact, though never explicitly stated, is the true meaning of the phrase 'fair trade'. The price relations prevailing in the importing country must be respected by raising the export price or cutting the volume of goods that is placed on that market.

LDCs have remained more unevenly integrated into world trade. Their exports are mostly concentrated in price-sensitive activities; their trade is still mainly of the inter-industrial kind, importing one kind of product, exporting another. The picture may be less static, it is true, than the one drawn here, especially as LDCs begin to form multinationals of their own so that trade and production become more integrated. In this way exports can be geared to particular uses or specific end-users, instead of being produced haphazardly for 'the market'.

At the risk of oversimplification, past experience has shown that trade opportunities can be expected to grow as business is conducted less and less at arm's length. It is only in textbooks that trade takes place exclusively among unrelated competitors. While free traders would exhort LDCs to 'get their prices right', one of the lessons that can be drawn from previous chapters is that this is only part of the picture. Firstly, prices must be competitive but not *too* competitive; secondly, besides the correct price structure, exports and marketing must be planned simultaneously, to enable suitable supply management.

The debate about the role of prices was also reflected in LAFTA, with polarization between those who believed that all that was necessary to get into the world market was to obtain a correct price structure and those who believed that production and trade had to be planned along complementary lines. Complementarity, however, was proved premature. To enable rationalization and supply management, it would have led to a cut in production rather than an increase in production, in contrast to the result that developed countries obtained with intra-industrial specialization. Intra-industrial specialization in this latter case had not needed to force cuts in production, rather it was able to offer consumers improved quality and increased variety. Where intra-industry specialization and oligopolistic market structures predominate, each producer is involved with one or a few sub-products that are unique in quality and price. Intra-industrial specialization among developed countries was made possible because of technological innovation and because economies of scale were realized before export markets were sought. Trade further released the potential for economies of scale, but the process was started before trade. In Latin America complementarity agreements were required to start from the opposite end; they sought to realize economies of scale with the wider markets made available by exports.

Whether in the old international division of labour (primary goods for manufacture) or in a new international division of labour (labour-intensive manufactures for capital-intensive goods), LDCs continue to sell their exports in competitive world markets while buying oligopolized markets. It is here also that the source of their weak bargaining power lies. Their exports are bound to encounter resistance since, as noted above, the implicit rule of international trade is that the prices prevailing in the importing country should not be undercut. So long as prices cannot be upset, companies operating from abroad can only aspire to a *part* of the domestic market. Otherwise they constitute a threat and will be treated as such.

The rule remained implicit among developed countries, who had similar price structures. It came to the fore in North–South relations. In the textile sector it was particularly blunt, with the notion of market disruption which specifically pointed to the problem caused by lower-priced imports. Had this been a more concentrated sector, exports could have been restricted or prices could have been raised unilaterally in order to respect the price relations in the importing countries. The 'global mushrooming' of textile production made that unfeasible. As the goods produced by countless suppliers are perfect substitutes and are produced for 'the market', concertation between producers was not possible. Such goods continue to be sold largely through intermediaries, be they importers or retail chains. Even in offshore processing, as was noted in Mexico's *maquila* exports and in the United States' 807.00

tariff provision, retailers have been comparatively more active and producing firms comparatively less than in the electrical and electronic goods sectors. Here the manufactures themselves have been the ones largely involved in subcontracting production abroad. In these cases trade is indeed motivated by price differentials, but these differentials, being captive within the established firms, are made to work to their advantage. Production is relocated but firms remain in business, internalizing the gains.

The different performance of sectors in the *maquila* indicate that, to assess the export prospects of LDCs, one can not merely look at conventional measures of their comparative advantage; the way in which production is organized worldwide is equally, if not more, relevant.

The extent to which the sector is internationalized and the degree of monopoly within the sector are also crucial variables in determining the shape of trade regulations. I have argued that textile production, being the most unconcentrated industrial sector, required a multilateral framework for the regulations to be effective. There are too many countries and too many firms within each country for any other form of concertation to be possible.[3] So far it has been the only sector to require monitoring under the GATT; one can speculate that it will remain unique in this respect. Other, more concentrated sectors can resort to less conspicuous ways of organizing trade or, better still, of organizing production so that problems may be ironed out as much as possible before they escalate onto the later stage of trading. High up on the concentration ladder is, for example, the aluminium industry: roughly three-quarters of the primary aluminium production of the Western world is owned wholly or in part by three American companies, Alcoa, Reynolds and Kaiser. These firms need not wait until the moment of trading; they can come to an agreement beforehand. Concentrated industries are able to fix up quotas and agreements on production, whereas in the case of unconcentrated industries, barriers to trade are set up.

The relevant distinction which follows from the degree of monopoly is, therefore, agreements regarding production versus agreements regarding trade. Once we reach the point where trade concertation becomes necessary, another qualitative distinction can be made, between bilateral and multi-lateral action, depending again on the degree of monopoly. If there are a limited number of producers involved, a bilateral solution may be all that is needed. Such is the case with steel, for example. Steel exports are carried out by a more limited number of countries and also by a more limited number of firms within each country. Orderly marketing agreements or voluntary export restraints can be negotiated on a country-to-country basis without the need for multilateral monitoring. On the bottom rung of the concentration ladder is the textile and clothing industry which for this reason needed GATT's authority to impose order in 'disrupted markets'. The analysis of the textile sector also brought to the fore the contradictions inherent in the foundations of the system built up on the free mobility of capital, though not of labour. The international market for labour perhaps shows most sharply the importance of political power when drawing the rules within which 'the free play of market forces' is allowed to operate. The developed countries, even at the height of their belief in *laissez faire*, have been less enthusiastic about labour than about capital mobility. In more recent years, international labour mobility has been tightened; when such mobility as there is bursts out of control, as is the case with Latin emigration to the United States, Asian emigration to Britain or African emigration to France, not only those prone to histrionics will remark that:

> the cries of alarm within the host country surpass in shrillness those of the most ardent Third World protectionist faced by smuggling. One need not be an expert in general equilibrium economic analysis to see that barriers to labour mobility will have a powerful effect on the whole configuration of world prices for goods and factors of production, i.e. on both world efficiency and income distribution. [Díaz Alejandro, 1983, p. 42.]

One conclusion that emerges from the study of the textile sector is that the wider the disparities in labour costs, the greater the pressure for protection. The rate of protection indicates the extent to which labour costs in the country's industry can exceed world market prices. The GATT contained no provisions to determine if and when import regulations might be justified to maintain a given level of wages. Countries finding themselves under this sort of pressure had to invent reasons. Such was the concept of 'market disruption'. The Nordic countries pioneered another makeshift concept, the need to maintain 'minimum viable production'; justifications for it were sought under the national security provisions of Article XXI, mainly because the GATT was found wanting in this respect (Dohlman, 1985).

Yet when the subject of these regulations was first mooted in the late-1950s, the measures were seen as temporary expedients that would gradually be removed as developed countries gave up their uncompetitive lines of production. Their full policy implications were not realized. The North–South debate owes its origin less to this issue than to import substitution and to its extension—regional integration. Here price considerations worked in the opposite direction. Regional integration was adversely judged if it was seen as fostering trade diversion, that is when a country dismissed price considerations to import from a higher-cost supplier after the formation of the free-trade area than before. Although, as was expected, when under scrutiny from the GATT, LAFTA members denied intentions of diverting trade, the protection of the area sought to offset the cost advantage of outsiders. It was in this respect that LDCs initially felt most bitter, probably because this was seen as having longer-term implications for development than the contemporaneous textile regulations which were seen as provisional. But the GATT was gradually adjusted to take into account the needs of import substitution. What the GATT could not do was to overcome its own birth defect, the widening differential in the mobility allowed to capital and labour. For import substitution and preference among LDCs, all that was needed was an acceptance of LDCs' self-imposed segregation from trade flows; trade among developed countries could continue unperturbed. However, the different mobility of capital and labour had implications for the integration of the LDCs with the developed countries.

A derivative of this basic inconsistency was a vision of trade divorced from money. Keynes had argued in his *Proposals for an International Clearing Union* that an unequal distribution of the world's money could prevent the principle of comparative advantage from operating. The GATT's normative view of trade essentially neglected their relationship, although one of its articles conceded that exceptional trade restrictions could be temporarily allowed for balance of payments reasons (Article XII). In the immediate post-war years, monetary reserves were concentrated in the United States and credit creation depended basically on the balance of payments deficits of the United States as a result of its capital exports and overseas military expenditure. The Latin American countries, largely left out of this circuit, and with deteriorating terms of trade, were short of finance. With the persistent tendency of imports to exceed exports, they were driven to rely on their domestic and regional markets. This is so even though the financial constraint was not the sole rationale for import substitution; these are also countries whose domestic markets are relatively large and the potential for import substitution therefore considerable. Only when a new financial circuit emerged with the expansion of international bank lending did other options become feasible.

Our discussion of the textile sector and regional market integration may lead to a gloomy view of prospects; yet the future need not be dismal. In the first place the problems encountered in these areas should not blind us to successes in others. These cases were chosen precisely because they were seen as problem areas. In the second place what has happened in the past is not an ordinance of nature and need not repeat itself. There are two strong temptations for researchers long involved in 'the search for pattern, regularity,order and principle' (Donelan, 1978, p. 14). One is to get caught in the web and feel that all policies are futile, that nothing can or will change. The other all-to-frequently followed temptation is to lock oneself securely in the ivory tower, and then self-righteously condemn policy-makers for not heeding priestly advice. Between the extremes of voluntarism and determinism there is, however, the middle-ground of uncertainty to be occupied by the cautious, the shy, the humble or the merely indecisive. The analysis of the preceding pages has held that the GATT was not instrumental for the growth of world trade. The GATT contributed an element of confidence and legitimacy to a process that would have occurred with or without it. The GATT merely enabled the growth to continue unabated. This view is further supported by the evidence of trade growth in services: it all began well before it was even discussed in the GATT.[4] Consequently, just as the GATT cannot claim the merit for the developed countries' trade growth, it cannot be blamed for LDCs' unsatisfactory performance. Likewise, LAFTA cannot be blamed for not promoting the growing market that ought to have been its foundation. LAFTA and its tariff agreements were wound up in 1980. What is to replace these agreements under LAIA is unclear. Yet despite uncertainty, regional imports have suffered less than imports from third countries in the face of the general contraction of credit and the consequent import squeeze. As Linder (1961) suggested, regarding the developed countries, success in catering for local markets has been the first step towards sustained export success. This, while being a necessary condition, is however not a sufficient condition for sustained export success. South–South trade, especially among some countries in Latin America, may have begun a phase of transition when, having attained the necessary condition, the sufficient condition, trade in virtually identical goods and oligopolistic markets, is still to be achieved. Whether this can be achieved without an adequately expanding domestic market brought about by income redistribution is debatable since the elasticity of demand for manufactures is markedly higher only once consumers move beyond the level of subsistence. South–South trade requires skilful economic planning and co-ordinated political will. Rewards will be reaped only bit by bit but the incrementalist process that is set into motion will undoubtedly contribute to offsetting the bias against LDCs in the international trading system. Policy-makers need to know what the real choices are in trade matters; yet they are still apt, as Keynes remarked, to be the mental prisoners of defunct economists.

The trade agreements signed by Argentina and Brazil in August 1986 will give optimists a sign of hope. The initiative draws the right lessons from past experience: it proposes a staged process of intra-industrial specialization in the capital goods sector and includes auxiliary agreements to facilitate payments and maintain the balance of trade in this area of manufactured goods.

Agnostics in academia may not necessarily be jubilant. Yet standing in the middle ground between determinism and voluntarism they also have a consolation: in sharing their doubts with their readers, they are suggesting new lines of progress in research. The thoughts offered here on the textile sector may suggest some potentially fruitful hypotheses. Industrial sectors move at different paces according to the interplay of three variables— internationalization, labour-intensity and concentration. It seems that the less internationalized and the more labour-intensive and unconcentrated production in a sector is, the more likely it is to be subject to tight trade regulation. Future research should try to show if and how this applies to other sectors.

The three variables are closely connected to technological change; its relation to trade is the other important door that has been left ajar.

NOTES

1. The interpretation of world trade offered in Chapter 3 dissents from this reasoning that economies of scale were caused primarily by exports. As argued there, exports were the culmination, not the beginning, of the process; they served to realize further the pre-existing potential for economies of scale.
2. There is a slight legal distinction between orderly marketing arrangements and voluntary export restraints. The first are agreements between governments and the latter are agreements between firms without the direct involvement of governments. The sort of bargaining that takes place can be clearly seen in the steel agreement reached in October 1982 between the EEC and the United States. The EEC agreed to limit its share of the American steel market to an average of 5.5 per cent compared to a share of 5.9 per cent in 1981. In exchange the United States withdrew countervailing action against European exporters.
3. Whether concertation is necessary from an outsider's point of view is another matter. The actors involved thought that it was.
4. Our reasoning would lead us to expect GATT to further liberalization in services with international production, oligopolized markets and technological special-ization, i.e. it will be easier in telecommunications than in transport.

Bibliography

A. SECONDARY WORKS

Alvares Maciel, G. 1977. *The International Framework for World Trade: Brazilian Proposals for GATT Reform*. London, Trade Policy Research Centre; also in *The World Economy*. Vol. 2, No. 1, January 1979.

Bagchi, A. K. 1982. *The Political Economy of Underdevelopment*. Cambridge, Cambridge University Press.

Balassa, B. 1965. 'Tariff Protection in Industrial Countries: An Evaluation'. *Journal of Political Economy*. Vol. 73, No. 4, December.

Ball, D. S. 1967. 'US Effective Tariffs and Labour's Share'. *Journal of Political Economy*. Vol. 75, No. 2, April.

Basevi, G. 1966. 'The US Tariff Structure: Estimates of Effective Rates of Protection of US Industries and Industrial Labour'. *Review of Economics and Statistics*. Vol. 48, May.

Behrman, J. 1972. *The Role of International Companies in Latin American Integration*. Lexington Mass., Lexington Books for the Committee for Economic Development.

Bergsten, C. F. 1975. 'On the Non-Equivalence of Import Quotas and Voluntary Export Restraints', in C. F. Bergsten (ed.), *Toward a New World Trade Policy: The Maidenhead Papers*. London, D.C. Heath & Co.

Bergsten, C. F. and Cline, W. R. 1982. *Trade Policy in the 1980s*. Washington DC, Institute for International Economics.

Bhagwati, J. 1965. 'On the Equivalence of Tariffs and Quotas', in R. Baldwin *et al.*, *Trade Growth and the Balance of Payments*. New York, Rand McNally.

Blackhurst, R., Marian, N. & Tumlir, J. 1977. *Trade Liberalisation, Protectionism and Interdependence*. Geneva, GATT Studies in International Trade.

Cable, V. 1983. *Protectionism and Industrial Decline*. London, Hodder & Stoughton.

Commonwealth Secretariat. 1982. *Protectionism: Threat to International Order. The Impact on Developing Countries*. London.

Cooper, R. N. 1973. 'Trade Policy is Foreign Policy', in R. N. Cooper (ed.), *A Reordered World*. Washington, DC, Potomac Associates.

Corden, W. M. 1965. *Recent Developments in the Theory of International Trade*. Special Papers in International Economics, No. 7, Princeton University.

Curzon, G. 1965. *Multilateral Commercial Diplomacy*. London, Michael Joseph.

Curzon, G. 1973. 'GATT: Traders Club', R. Cox & H. Jacobson (eds), *The Anatomy of Influence: Decision-making in International Organizations*. New Haven and London, Yale University Press.

Curzon G. & V. 1976. 'The Management of Trade Relations in the GATT', in A. Shonfield, *International Economic Relations of the Western World, Vol. I*. London, Oxford University Press for Royal Institute of International Affairs.

Dam, K. 1970. *The GATT: Law and International Organization*. Chicago, University of Chicago Press.

Dell, S. 1966. *A Latin American Common Market?* London, Oxford University Press.
Destler, I. M. *et al.* 1979. *The Textile Wrangle: Conflict in Japanese–American Relations, 1969–71.* Ithaca, London, Cornell University Press.
De Vries, B. A. 1977. 'Exports in the New World Environment'. *CEPAL Review*, No. 3, April.
Díaz Alejandro, C. F. 1975. 'Trade Policies and Economic Development', in P. B. Kenen (ed.), *International Trade and Finance: Frontiers for Research*. Cambridge, Mass., Harvard University Press.
Díaz Alejandro, C. F. 1983. 'Open Economy, Close Polity', in D. Tussie (ed.), *Latin America in the World Economy*. Aldershot, Gower.
Díaz Alejandro, C. F. & Helleiner, G. 1983. *Handmaiden in Distress*. Washington, DC, Overseas Development Council, London, Overseas Development Institute and Ottawa, North–South Institute.
Dillman, C. D. 1983. 'Assembly Industries in Mexico', *Journal of Interamerican and World Affairs*, Vol. 25, No. 1, February.
Dohlman E. 1985. *Swedish Foreign Trade Policy and National Security*. Ph.D. thesis, London School of Economics.
Donelan, M. D. 1978. 'Introduction', in M. D. Donelan (ed.), *The Reason of States: A Study in International Political Theory*. London, Allen & Unwin.
Dunning, J. 1970. *Studies in International Investment*, London, Allen & Unwin.
Dunning, J. 1973. 'The Determinants of International Production', *Oxford Economic Papers*. Vol. 25, No. 1, March.
Evans, J. 1971. *The Kennedy Round in American Trade Policy: The Twilight of the GATT*. Cambridge, Mass., Harvard University Press.
Evans, P. B. 1979. *Dependent Development: The Alliance of Multinational, State and Local Capital in Brazil*. Princeton, NJ, Princeton University Press.
Finch, M. H. J. 1982. 'The Latin American Free Trade Association', in A. M. El-Agraa (ed.), *International Economic Integration*. London and Basingstoke, Macmillan.
Finger, J. M. 1975. 'Tariff Provisions for Offshore Assembly and Exports of Developing Countries', *The Economic Journal*, Vol. 85, June.
Fitzgerald, E. V. K. 1983. 'The State and the Management of Accumulation in the Periphery', in D. Tussie (ed.), *Latin America in the World Economy*. Aldershot, Gower.
Frank, A. G. 1969. *Capitalism and Underdevelopment: Historical Studies of Chile and Brazil*. New York and London, Monthly Review Press.
Froebel, F., Heinrichs, J. & Kreye, O. 1980. *The New International Division of Labour*, Cambridge, Cambridge University Press.
Gardner, R. 1969. *Sterling–Dollar Diplomacy: the Origins and Prospects of Our International Economic Order*. New York, McGraw Hill.
Golt, S. 1978. *Developing Countries in the GATT System*. London, Thames Essay 13, Trade Policy Research Centre.
Gosovic, B., *UNCTAD: Conflict and Compromise*, Leiden, A. W. Sijthoff, 1972.
Griffith-Jones, S. 'The Growth of Transnational Finance: Implications for National Development', in D. Tussie (ed.), *Latin America in the World Economy*. Aldershot, Gower.
Grubel, H. & Lloyd, P. 1975. *Intraindustry Trade*, London, Macmillan for Trade Policy Research Centre.
Helleiner, G. 1981. *Intrafirm Trade and the Developing Countries*. London, Macmillan.
Henderson, H. 1949. 'The Havana Charter', *American Economic Review*. Vol. 39, June.
Hindley, B. 1980. 'Voluntary Export Restraints and the GATT's Main Escape Clause', *The World Economy*. Vol. 3, No. 3, November.
Hirschman, A. 1971. 'The Political Economy of Import Substitution in Latin America',

in A. Hirschman, *A Bias for Hope: Essays on Development and Latin America*, London and New Haven, Yale University Press.

Huber, J. 1981. 'The Practice of GATT in Examining Regional Arrangements under Art. XXIV'. *Journal of Common Market Studies*. Vol. 19, No. 3, March.

Hymer, S. 1976. *The International Operations of National Firms*. Cambridge, Mass., MIT.

Joekes, S. 1982. 'The MFA and Outward Processing: the Case of Morocco and Tunisia', in C. Stevens (ed.), *The EEC and the Third World: A Survey, 2*. London, Overseas Development Institute and Brighton, Institute of Development Studies.

Keesing, D. B. 1977. 'Recent Trends in Manufactured and Total Exports from Developing Countries'. Washington DC, World Bank, June, mimeo.

Keesing, D. B. & Wolf, M. 1980. *Textiles Quotas Against Developing Countries*, London, Trade Policy Research Centre.

Kenwood, A. G. & Lougheed, A. L. 1983. *The Growth of the International Economy 1820–1980*. London, Allen & Unwin.

Kindleberger, C. *Government and International Trade*. Essays in International Finance, No. 129, Princeton University, July.

Kock, K. 1969. *International Trade Policy and the GATT 1947–67*. Stockholm, Almqvist Wiksell.

Kojima, K. 1975. 'A Macroeconmic Theory of Foreign Direct Investment', in C. F. Bergsten (ed.), *Toward a New World Trade Policy: The Maidenhead Papers*. London, D. C. Heath & Co.

Krueger, A. O. 1978. *Foreign Trade Regimes and Economic Development: Liberalisation Attempts and Consequences*. New York, Ballinger Publishing Co. for National Bureau of Economic Research.

Lewis, W. A. 1949. *Economic Survey 1919–1939*. London, Allen & Unwin.

Lewis, W. A. 1977. *The Evolution of the International Economic Order*. Princeton, NJ, Princeton University Press.

Linder, S. B. 1961. *An Essay on Trade and Transformation*. Uppsala, Almqvist & Wiksell.

Linder, S. B. 1964. 'The Significance of GATT for Underdeveloped Countries', in *Proceedings of the United Nations Conference on Trade and Development*. New York.

List F. 1974. *National System of Political Economy*. New York and London, Garland Publishing, Inc.

Lortie, P. 1975. *Economic Integration and the Law of GATT*, New York, Praeger.

Maizels, A. 1963. *Industrial Growth and World Trade: An Empirical Study of Trends in Production, Consumption and Trade in Manufactures from 1899 to 1959*. Cambridge, Cambridge University Press.

Meltzer, R. I. 1975. *The Politics of Policy Reversal: The American Response to the Issue of Granting Preferences to the Developing Countries, 1964–67*, unpublished Ph.D. dissertation, Columbia University.

Meyer, F. V. 1978. *International Trade Policy*. London, Croom Helm.

Mill, J. S. 1965. *Principles of Political Economy* (1848), *Collected works by J. S. Mill*. Toronto, University of Toronto Press and London, Routledge & Kegan Paul.

Morawetz, D. 1982. *Why the Emperor's New Clothes are not Made in Colombia*. New York, Oxford University Press for World Bank.

Myint, H. 1969. 'International Trade and the Developing Countries', in P. A. Samuelson (ed.), *International Economic Relations: Proceedings of the Third Congress of the International Economic Association*. London, MacMillan and New York, St. Martin's.

Myrdal, G. 1956. *An International Economy: Problems and Prospects*. London, Routledge & Kegan Paul.

Ozawa, T. 1979. *Multinationalism, Japanese Style: The Political Economy of Outward Dependency*. Princeton, NJ, Princeton University Press.

Patterson, G. 1966. *Discrimination in International Trade: The Policy Issues, 1945–1965*. Princeton, NJ, Princeton University Press.

Pelzman, J. 1982. 'The Textile Industry', *The Annals of the American Academy of Political Social Science*. Vol. 460, March.

Perry, G. 1982. 'World Markets for Manufactures and Industrialisation in Developing Countries', in R. Ffrench-Davis & E. Tironi (eds), *Latin America and the New International Economic Order*. London, Macmillan.

Prebisch, R. 1982. 'Five Stages in my Thinking on Development', Washington DC, World Bank, mimeo.

Prebisch, R., Herrera, F., Sanz De Santamaria, C. & Mayobre, J. A. 1966. 'Proposals for the Creation of a Latin American Common Market', reproduced in S. Dell, *A Latin American Common Market?* London, Oxford University Press.

Preeg, E. H. 1970. *Traders and Diplomats: An Analysis of the Kennedy Round of Negotiations under the General Agreement on Tariffs and Trade*. Washington, DC, The Brookings Institution.

Salgado, G. 1979. 'The Latin American Regional Market: The Project and the Reality'. *CEPAL Review* No. 7, April.

Saunders, C. 1975. *From Free Trade to Integration*. London, Royal Institute of International Affairs and Political and Economic Planning, January.

Shonfield, A. (ed). 1976. *International Economic Relations of the Western World. Vol. I. Politics and Trade*. London, Oxford University Press for Royal Institute of International Affairs.

Singer, H. 1950. 'The Distribution of Gains between Investing and Borrowing Countries', *American Economic Review, Papers and Proceedings*. Vol. 11, No. 2; also in H. Singer (1978).

Singer, H. 1978. *The Structure of International Development: Essays on the Economics of Backwardness*. London, Macmillan.

Singer, H. & Ansari, J. 1977. *Rich and Poor Countries*. London, Allen & Unwin.

Smith, A. *An Enquiry into the Nature and Causes of the Wealth of Nations*, 1776, Glasgow.

Stein, L. 1984. *Trade and Structural Change*. London, Croom Helm.

Stewart, F. 1976. 'The Direction of International Trade: Gains and Losses for the Third World', in G. Helleiner (ed.), *A World Divided: The Less Developed Countries in the International Economy*, Cambridge, Cambridge University Press.

Stolper, W. 1949. 'Problems of the International Trade Organization. Discussion'. *American Economic Review Supplement*, Vol. 39, May.

Strange, S. 1979. 'The Management of Surplus Capacity: or How Does Theory Stand up to Protectionism 1970s Style?' *International Organization*, Vol. 33.3, Summer.

Strange, S. & Tooze, R. (eds), 1981. *The International Politics of Surplus Capacity*. London, Allen & Unwin.

Thorp, R. & Whitehead, L. (eds), 1979. *Inflation and Stabilisation in Latin America*. London, Macmillan.

Tumlir, J. 1979. 'The New Protectionism, Cartels and the International Order', in R. Amacher, G. Haberler & T. Willet (eds), *Challenges to a Liberal International Economic Order*. Washington, DC, American Enterprise Institute.

Vaitsos, C. 1980. 'Corporate Integration in World Production and Trade', in C. Vaitsos & D. Seers (eds), *Integration and Unequal Development: The Experience of the EEC*, London, Macmillan.

Vernon, R. 1971. *Sovereignty at Bay: The Multinational Spread of US Enterprise*. New York, Basic Books.

Viner, J. 1950. *The Customs Union Issue*. London, Stevens & Sons.

Wilcox, C. 1949. *A Charter for World Trade*. New York, Macmillan.

Wionczek, M. 1966. 'Requisites for Viable Integration', in M. Wionczek (ed.), *Latin American Economic Integration*. New York, Praeger.
Wolf, M. 1981. 'Issues in the MFA Negotiations'. London, Trade Policy Research Centre, mimeo.

B. OFFICIAL DOCUMENTS AND PUBLICATIONS

1. GATT publications

Basic Instruments and Selected Documents (BISD)
Com. TD/100
Focus Newsletter
L/documents
Press releases
Proceedings of Ministerial Meetings
SR/documents
The Tokyo Round of Multilateral Trade Negotiations, April 1979
Trends in International Trade, Report by a Panel of Experts, 1958

2. Other official documents and publications

Argentine Republic (see also Republica Argentina), *Economic Information on Argentina*
Comité International de la Rayonne et des Fibres Synthétiques, *The Future of the Man-Made Fibre Industry in Western Europe*, Paris, 1976
Consejo Argentino para las Relaciones Internacionales, *La Argentina y el Proceso de Reestructuración de la Asociación Latinoamericana de Libre Comercio*, Buenos Aires, 1979
Courtaulds, *Annual Reports*
Dupont Corporation, *Annual Reports*
Economic Commission for Latin America (ECLA), *Economic Bulletin for Latin America*, various issues
Economic Commission for Latin America (ECLA), *Economic Survey for Latin America*, various issues
Economic Commission for Latin America (ECLA), *The Latin American Common Market*, United Nations Sales, No. 59.II. G.4, Mexico DF, July 1959
Economic Commission for Latin America (ECLA), *Press releases*
European Economic Community, Commission, *Communication to the Council Report on Two Years Operation of the Multifibre Agreement*, Brussels, 1979
European Economic Community, Commission, *Proposals to the Council*, Com (79), 32 final, Brussels, 1979
Instituto para la Integración de America Latina (INTAL), *Revista de Integración Latino-americana*, various issues
Instituto para la Integración de America Latina (INTAL), Inv/12/dtl, Buenos Aires, 1968
Instituto para la Integración de America Latina (INTAL), *La integración economica en America Latina*, Beunos Aires, 1968
Interamerican Development Bank (IDB), *Economic and Social Progress in Latin America*, Washington DC, 1979
International Federation of Cotton and Allied Textile Industries, *Annual Conference*, Zurich, 1976

International Monetary Fund, *Developments in International Trade Policy*, Occasional Paper 16, Washington DC, 1982

Repùblica Argentina, Presidencia de la Nación, *Plan de reestablecimiento económico* (by R. Prebisch), Beunos Aires, January 1956

United Nations, *The Economic Development of Latin America and its Principal Problems* (by R. Prebisch), E/CN.12/89/Rev. 1, New York, 1950

United Nations, *Multinational Corporations in World Development*, New York, 1973

United Nations Conference on Trade and Development, *Fibres and Textiles: Dimensions of Corporate Marketing Structure*, TD/B/C.1/219, Geneva, 1980

United Nations Conference on Trade and Development, *International Trade in Cotton Textiles and the Developing Countries: Problems and Prospects*, TD/BN/C.2/117/Rev. 1, Geneva, 1974

United Nations Conference on Trade and Development, *Measures for Expansion of Markets in Developed Countries for the Exports of Manufactures and Semi-manufactures of Developing Countries*, E.CON/46/PC/20, Geneva, 1974

United Nations Conference on Trade and Development, MTN/CB.22, Geneva, 20 October, 1980 (Conf)

United Nations Conference on Trade and Development, *Multilateral Trade Negotiations: Evolution and Further Recommendations Arising Therefrom*, TD/227/Add 1, Manila, 7 May 1979

United Nations Conference on Trade and Development, *Proceedings of the United Nations Conference on Trade and Development*, New York, 1964

United Nations Conference on Trade and Development, *Protectionism, Trade Relations and Structural Adjustment*, TD/274, Belgrade, June 1983

United Nations Conference on Trade and Development, *The Kennedy Round: Preliminary Evaluation of the Results with Special Reference to Developing Countries*, TD/6, Geneva, 1967

United Nations Conference on Trade and Development, *The Role of Transnational Enterprises in Latin American Economic Integration Efforts: Who Integrates, and With Whom, How and for Whose Benefit?*, ST/ECDC/19, New York, 1982

United Nations Conference on Trade and Development, *Trade and Development Report 1981*, Geneva, 1981

United States Department of Commerce, International Trade Administration, *News Releases*, Washington DC

United States, Department of State, *Proposals for the Expansion of World Trade and Employment* (Clayton Plan), Publication 2411, Commercial Policy Series, 79, Washington DC, 1945

United States, Department of State, *Suggested Charter for an International Trade Organization of the United Nations*, Publication 2598, Commercial Policy Series 93, Washington DC, 1946

United States, International Trade Commission, *The History and Current Status of the Multifiber Arrangement*, Publication 850, Washington DC, January 1978

United States, International Trade Commission, *The Multifiber Arrangement 1973–1980*, Publication 1131, Washington DC, March 1983

United States, Senate, *Implications of Multinational Firms for World Trade and Investments and for US Trade and Labor*. Report to the Committee on Finance and Subcommittee on International Trade on Investigation No. 332–69 under Section 332 of the Tariff Act 1930, Washington DC, February 1973

World Bank (International Bank for Reconstruction and Development), *Private Foreign Direct Investment in Developing Countries*, Staff Working Paper, No. 348, 1979

C. PERIODICAL PUBLICATIONS

Business Latin America
The Economist
El Cronista Comercial
Europe Information, *The EEC and the Textile Arrangements*, Brussels, 1978
European Report No. 470, Brussels, 17 December 1977
Finance & Development
The Financial Times
Fortune
The Guardian
Hechos e Ideas
Revista de Integración Latinoamericana
South
Textile Asia

Index

India (*cont.*)
  export control system 95
  industrialization in 18, 19
  as member of GATT 26, 27, 28, 30
  textile sector trade 65, 76, 78
Indonesia 18, 26, 27, 98, 128
industrial convergence 39–42, 43, 44, 49, 57
Industrial Revolution, and textiles 7
industrialization, by LDCs 18–19, 21–2, 32–3, 109
infant industry argument for protection 20–1, 137
Inter-American Development Bank *see* IDB
inter-industrial trade 45, 58
International Bank for Reconstruction and Development *see* IBRD
international investment 48, 49, 58, 60–1
international labour market 61
International Monetary Fund *see* IMF
international specialization and growth of international trade 6, 38, 58, 73, 91, 136–7, 139
international trade, growth of
  capital mobility and 5, 48
  commodity composition of 45, 57
  concentration in developed countries 57
  decline of in 1930s 9
  intra-industry trade and 5
  oligopolistic nature of 5
  not essentially ruled by price competition 5
  protectionism and 81–2
  role of GATT in assessed 144–5
International Trade, Note on the Expansion of (GATT) 26–7, 28
International Trade Organization *see* ITO
internationalization
  of capital 52–4, 58–9, 86
  of production 46–52, 90
  as share of exports 47
intra-firm specialization 52
intra-firm trade 53, 54, 55, 58, 86, 139
intra-industry specialization 63 (n 3), 82, 90, 139
intra-industry trade 49, 139
  complementarity agreements in Latin America 114
  definition of 40
  economies of scale and 44
  GATT and 45–6
  and growth of international trade 5
  and industrial convergence 39–42, 43, 57
  in Japan and Southeast Asia 89
  in Latin America 124
  in off-shore processing 55
  R & D-intensive sectors and 43, 44, 82
  specialization and 44
  tariff reduction and 82

  in Western Europe 115–17
Israel 27
Italy 41, 47, 59, 84
ITO (International Trade Organization) 20, 105, 136
  objects and origins 1, 11
  non-ratification by United States 12, 77

Japan 58
  and accession to GATT 15, 68, 77
  discrimination against 33
  electronic sector in 53–4, 59
  exports 68–9, 78, 89
  foreign direct investment by 48, 49, 88–9, 100
  international production as share of exports 47
  intra-industrial trade 41
  machine tool exports to EEC 94, 95
  preferential systems 31
  textile trade and LTA/MFA 64, 65, 68, 72, 75–9
  voluntary export quotas 68, 77, 88
Joekes, S. 57
joint ventures 59

Kaiser company 142
Keesing, D. B. 7, 104
Keesing, D. B. and Wolf, M. 68, 75, 78, 80, 85, 89
Kennedy, President John F. 78
Kenwood, A. G. and Lougheed, A. L. 9, 45
Keynes, J. M. 2, 11, 22, 145
  International Clearing Union 10, 144
Kindleburger, C. 80
Knight, Sir Arthur vii
Kock, K. 2, 4, 19, 105
Kojima, K. 50, 87, 88
Krueger, Anne O. 122, 124

Labour costs 61, 85, 90
  market disruption and 73, 86, 143
  and complementarity 114, 116, 128, 133
  establishment of 7, 105, 107, 112
  failure of 125, 127, 133
  international monetary reserves 122–3
  margins of preference 124–7, 133
  MFN rule 128
  principal supplier and reciprocity rules 27
LAIA (Latin American Integration Association) 127, 128–31, 145
Laos 128
LAFTA (Latin America Free Trade Area) 7–8, 36, 51, 64, 111, 138, 143, 145
Latin America, regional integration in 104–33, 143, 144